The Most Famous Speeches of Abraham Lincoln: The History of the Cooper Union Address, the Gettysburg Address, and the Second Inaugural Address

By Charles River Editors

A picture of Lincoln taken in New York City in 1860

About Charles River Editors

Charles River Editors provides superior editing and original writing services across the digital publishing industry, with the expertise to create digital content for publishers across a vast range of subject matter. In addition to providing original digital content for third party publishers, we also republish civilization's greatest literary works, bringing them to new generations of readers via ebooks.

Sign up here to receive updates about free books as we publish them, and visit Our Kindle Author Page to browse today's free promotions and our most recently published Kindle titles.

Introduction

David Shankbone's picture of Cooper Union in 2007

The Cooper Union Address (February 1860)

"It is surely safe to assume that the thirty-nine framers of the original Constitution, and the seventy-six members of the Congress which framed the amendments thereto, taken together, do certainly include those who may be fairly called "our fathers who framed the Government under which we live." And so assuming, I defy any man to show that any one of them ever, in his whole life, declared that, in his understanding, any proper division of local from federal authority, or any part of the Constitution, forbade the Federal Government to control as to slavery in the federal territories." – Abraham Lincoln

"[O]ne of the most happiest and most convincing political arguments ever made in this City ... No man ever made such an impression on his first appeal to a New-York audience." – Horace

Greeley

After the Lincoln-Douglas debates made Lincoln a nationally recognized politician, Illinois papers began to mention Lincoln as a Republican candidate for President throughout 1859. Lincoln was humbled, though a bit dumbfounded. He thought himself more suited for the Senate, where he could orate and discuss ideas, and moreover there were Republicans of much greater national prominence on the East coast, particularly William Seward. Lacking any administrative experience, he wasn't sure he would enjoy being President, but even being considered was a great honor, and he quietly thought the idea over.

In fact, Lincoln was still not considered a real option for the nomination until he delivered a speech at New York City's Cooper Union in February 1860, just a few months before the Republicans' convention in May. Lincoln had gained a bit of a national profile by debating Stephen Douglas during an Illinois Senate Race in 1858, and though he lost that election, Lincoln continued discussing the same themes, most notably slavery and *Dred Scott* in his Cooper Union speech. In the hard-hitting speech, Lincoln both deflected Southern criticisms and attacked them, chiding would-be secessionists, "Your purpose, then, plainly stated, is that you will destroy the Government, unless you be allowed to construe and enforce the Constitution as you please, on all points in dispute between you and us. You will rule or ruin in all events."

Although just 7,000 words long, the Cooper Union Address was almost universally praised in the North, and biographer Harold Holzer credited it for leading Lincoln to the presidency: "Had Abraham Lincoln failed at his do-or-die debut in New York, he would never have won his party's presidential nomination three months later, not to mention election to the White House that November. Such was the impact of a triumph in the nation's media capital. Had he stumbled, none of the challenges that roiled his presidency would ever have tested his iron will… He had arrived at Cooper Union a politician with more defeats than victories, but he departed politically reborn."

Going into the convention that May, the Republicans were hopeful; the Democratic Party, partly because of Stephen Douglas, was deeply divided over slavery, and it had broken into a Northern and Southern faction. By dividing their votes, they were likely handing over the presidency to a Republican Party that would barely win a plurality across the nation. Sensing opportunity, the Republicans were careful in selecting their candidate. Many delegates considered the frontrunner, William H. Seward, to be too radical. With a divided electorate, there were fears that Seward's radicalism might lose the Midwest for the Republicans. At the convention, Seward's support maintained steady throughout the rounds of voting, but Lincoln polled a surprising second place on the first ballot, and he gradually picked up votes from others until he was selected as the Republican Party's nominee on the third ballot.

This book chronicles the history of the speech from its origins to its legacy. Along with pictures of important people, places, and events, you will learn about the Cooper Union Address like never before.

The Gettysburg Address

Lincoln at the dedication ceremony in November 1863

"Four score and seven years ago our fathers brought forth on this continent a new nation, conceived in liberty, and dedicated to the proposition that all men are created equal. Now we are engaged in a great civil war, testing whether that nation, or any nation so conceived and so dedicated, can long endure. We are met on a great battlefield of that war. We have come to dedicate a portion of that field, as a final resting place for those who here gave their lives that that nation might live." – Abraham Lincoln

Without question, the most famous battle of the American Civil War took place outside of the small town of Gettysburg, Pennsylvania, which happened to be a transportation hub, serving as the center of a wheel with several roads leading out to other Pennsylvanian towns. From July 1-

3, Robert E. Lee's Confederate Army of Northern Virginia tried everything in its power to decisively defeat George Meade's Union Army of the Potomac, unleashing ferocious assaults that inflicted nearly 50,000 casualties in all.

After the South had lost the war, the importance of Gettysburg as one of the "high tide" marks of the Confederacy became apparent to everyone, making the battle all the more important in the years after it had been fought. While former Confederate generals cast about for scapegoats, with various officers pointing fingers at Robert E. Lee, James Longstreet, and James Stuart, historians and avid Civil War fans became obsessed with studying and analyzing all the command decisions and army movements during the entire campaign. Despite the saturation of coverage, Americans refuse to grow tired of visiting the battlefield and reliving the biggest battle fought in North America.

When a crowd came to Gettysburg in November 1863 to commemorate the battle fought there 4 months earlier and dedicate a new national cemetery, they came to hear a series of speeches about the Civil War and the events of that battle. Today it may seem obvious to invite the president to such an occasion, but Lincoln was initially an afterthought, and though he did come to deliver remarks, he was not in fact the keynote speaker. Instead, the man chosen to give the keynote speech was Edward Everett, a politician and educator from Massachusetts. Everett had already been a Congressman, the 15th Governor of Massachusetts, Minister to Great Britain, and Secretary of State, and by the Civil War, he was considered perhaps the greatest orator in the nation, making him a natural choice to be the featured speaker at the dedication ceremony.

Everett is still known today for his oratory, but more for the fact that he spoke for over two hours at Gettysburg immediately before President Lincoln delivered his immortal two-minute Gettysburg Address. Everett would later say, "I should be glad if I could flatter myself that I came as near to the central idea of the occasion, in two hours, as you did in two minutes." At the time, however, Lincoln and many others present at the event thought his speech fell flat and was ultimately a failure that would be consigned to the dustbin of history.

Perhaps Lincoln's most impressive feat is that he was able to convey so much with so few words; after Everett spoke for hours at Gettysburg, Lincoln's Gettysburg Address only took a few minutes, but in those few minutes, Lincoln invoked the principles of human equality espoused by the Declaration of Independence. In the process, he redefined the Civil War as a struggle not merely for the Union but as "a new birth of freedom" that would bring true equality to all of its citizens, ensure that democracy would remain a viable form of government, and would also create a unified nation in which states' rights were no longer dominant.

150 years later, Lincoln's speech is still considered arguably the greatest in American history, yet the exact wording of the speech is disputed. The five known manuscripts of the Gettysburg Address differ in a number of details and also differ from contemporary newspaper reprints of the speech. In fact, at the time, few Americans knew the president had even given a speech at

Gettysburg, and the Gettysburg Address was not widely covered in newspapers. The irony is lost on few, given that the Gettysburg Address continues to represent a concise and eloquent statement on the very purpose of the United States.

This book chronicles the history of the speech from its origins to its legacy. Along with pictures of important people, places, and events, you will learn about the Gettysburg Address like never before.

Lincoln's Second Inaugural Address

A picture of the Second Inaugural Address

"With malice toward none, with charity for all, with firmness in the right as God gives us to see the right, let us strive on to finish the work we are in, to bind up the nation's wounds, to care for him who shall have borne the battle and for his widow and his orphan, to do all which may achieve and cherish a just and lasting peace among ourselves and with all nations." – Abraham Lincoln

When Abraham Lincoln decisively won reelection in 1864, he began working speedily towards finishing the war and figuring out its aftermath. With this clear mandate for governing, the

Republicans in the House, with Lincoln's support, approved of the 13th Amendment to the Constitution, which banned slavery in all territories and states. In addition to the 13th Amendment, the future 14th and 15th Amendments to the Constitution were being discussed to protect minorities as well. To assist freed slaves, Congress also created the Freedmen's Bureau to offer food, clothing and shelter to former slaves in the South. Lincoln did his part as well, issuing a Proclamation for Amnesty and Reconstruction, which offered full pardons and amnesty to all Rebels, except those high level officials involved in governing the Confederacy.

In Lincoln's mind, since the South had never legally seceded, forgiveness was to be his top priority. He wanted to allow states to be readmitted to the Union after only 10% of its citizens swore an oath of loyalty to the United States. It was apparent that Lincoln envisioned a relatively short-lived Reconstruction process in which the former Confederate states would draft constitutions and rejoin the Union. He thought (or at least hoped) the country could effectively continue operating much as it had before the Civil War, but his vision would remain just a dream when his life, and thus his role in Reconstruction, was cut short just days after Lee surrendered to Grant at Appomattox.

Lincoln wasn't given a chance to finish his work, but his thoughts and visions were eloquently saved for posterity in his second inaugural address, delivered a month before his death and considered one of America's greatest speeches. With the war nearing the end, Lincoln struck a conciliatory tone, reminding both sides that they prayed to the same God for victory and that neither side could divine God's will. "With malice toward none, with charity for all," Lincoln called for peace and reunion, his eye clearly on Reconstruction.

By pointing to the two sides' similarities, Lincoln aimed to remind the divided nation that they were all Americans, but the speech also alluded to religious sentiments that were often not present in Lincoln's words. In fact, one of the methods in which Lincoln struck a conciliatory tone was by reminding the Union that they were no more an authority of God's will than the Confederates: "Both read the same Bible and pray to the same God, and each invokes His aid against the other. It may seem strange that any men should dare to ask a just God's assistance in wringing their bread from the sweat of other men's faces, but let us judge not, that we be not judged. The prayers of both could not be answered."

Nobody will ever know if Lincoln could've managed the Reconstruction process in a better way than what actually unfolded, but in many respects, the second inaugural address was a fitting postscript of sorts to his presidency. Ironically, the crowd of over 50,000 spectators included John Wilkes Booth, who can actually be seen in the most familiar picture of the speech at the unfinished U.S. Capitol Building. Alongside Booth in the audience were several of his eventual co-conspirators: Samuel Arnold, George Atzerodt, David Herold, Michael O'Laughlen, Lewis Powell and John Surratt. All of the conspirators were either from or lived in the Washington, D.C. area or in Maryland, and all were opposed to President Lincoln and were fervent supporters of the Confederates.

This book chronicles the history of the speech from its origins to its legacy. Along with pictures of important people, places, and events, you will learn about the Second Inaugural Address like never before.

The Most Famous Speeches of Abraham Lincoln: The History of the Cooper Union Address, the Gettysburg Address, and the Second Inaugural Address

The Cooper Union Address

Chapter 1: 19ᵗʰ Century Politics

"Abolitionism proposes to destroy the right and extinguish the principle of self-government for which our forefathers waged a seven years' bloody war, and upon which our whole system of free government is founded." – Senator Stephen Douglas, 1854.

When President Thomas Jefferson went ahead with the Louisiana Purchase, he wasn't entirely sure what was on the land he was buying, or whether the purchase was even constitutional. Ultimately, the Louisiana Purchase encompassed all or part of 15 current U.S. states and two Canadian provinces, including Arkansas, Missouri, Iowa, Oklahoma, Kansas, Nebraska, parts of Minnesota that were west of the Mississippi River, most of North Dakota, nearly all of South Dakota, northeastern New Mexico, northern Texas, the portions of Montana, Wyoming, and Colorado east of the Continental Divide, and Louisiana west of the Mississippi River, including the city of New Orleans. In addition, the Purchase contained small portions of land that would eventually become part of the Canadian provinces of Alberta and Saskatchewan. The purchase, which immediately doubled the size of the United States at the time, still comprises around 23% of current American territory.

With so much new territory to carve into states, the balance of Congressional power became a hot topic in the decade after the purchase, especially when the people of Missouri sought to be admitted to the Union in 1819 with slavery being legal in the new state. While Congress was dealing with that, Alabama was admitted in December 1819, creating an equal number of free states and slave states. Thus, allowing Missouri to enter the Union as a slave state would disrupt the balance.

James Tallmadge of New York was the first to try to address this issue by limiting slavery in Missouri, and the Tallmadge Amendment sought to ensure that children of slave parents born in Missouri would automatically go free at the age of 25: ""And provided, That the further introduction of slavery or involuntary servitude be prohibited, except for the punishment of crimes, whereof the party shall have been fully convicted; and that all children born within the said State, after the admission thereof into the Union, shall be free at the age of twenty-five years." While the House passed legislation with that amendment in it, the Senate refused to go along with it.

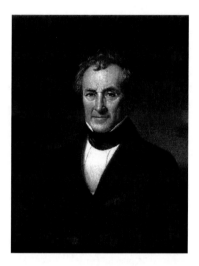

Tallmadge

The Senate ultimately got around this issue by establishing what became known as the Missouri Compromise. Legislation was passed that admitted Maine as a free state, thus balancing the number once Missouri joined as a slave state. Moreover, slavery would be excluded from the Missouri Territory north of the parallel 36°30′ north, which was the southern border of Missouri itself. As a slave state, Missouri would obviously serve as the lone exception to that line.

The Missouri Compromise of 1820 staved off the crisis for the time being, but by setting a line that excluded slave states above the parallel, it would also become incredibly contentious. In 1831, the South was suffering under the harsh effects of the Tariff of 1828, which had been passed during the presidency of John Quincy Adams. The tariff taxed the importation of manufactured goods, many of which came from the industries of Great Britain, with the intention of protecting industry in the Northern states from competition from foreign industrial countries. The South, however, was less industrial and relied on the export of cotton; by reducing the competitiveness of British industry, the economy there was less able to afford to import cotton from the United States. To the South, the protective tariffs were one-sided and supported the North at the expense of the South, and the region loudly opposed them.

Congress worked to soften and reduce the impact of the tariff with the Tariff of 1832, which was less harsh than the one from 1828, but the South still opposed the bill. In response, South Carolina began to consider passing an ordinance of nullification, prohibiting the tariff within its borders. Vice President John C. Calhoun encouraged the act and supported its constitutionality. On November 19th, South Carolina adopted the Ordinance of Nullification, overturning the tariffs of 1828 and 1832 within its borders. It also vowed that any attempts to enforce the law within its borders would lead to the state's secession from the Union.

Modern American jurisprudence has ensured that federal laws are supreme to state laws when they are in conflict, but South Carolina's assertion that it had the ability to nullify a federal law dated all the way back to the "Kentucky and Virginia Resolutions", which were drafted by Jefferson and Madison. Together, the two drafted the first major political documents advocating the rights of the states to nullify federal law that the states believed was unconstitutional. Citing this doctrine of "nullification," various states in both the North and South asserted the states' rights to consider federal laws invalid. The Resolutions sought to nullify the Alien and Sedition Acts within those states back in the late 18th century, Northern states debated nullification during the War of 1812, and in 1860, Southern states would take nullification one step further to outright secession, leading to the Civil War.

Amid the crisis, President Andrew Jackson was reelected by a wide margin. He did not, however, win the state of South Carolina, which nominated its own candidate, John Floyd of the Nullifier Party. Within less than a week of his reelection, Jackson stated his position on the Nullification Crisis, asserting that the doctrine of Nullification was an "impractical absurdity," defied Constitutional law, and was tantamount to treason. President Jackson absolutely denied that a state had the right to overturn federal law, and he committed the U.S. military to quelling any attempts to do that in South Carolina. Ten days later, Vice President Calhoun resigned, having won a seat in the U.S. Senate, and he continued to support Nullification throughout the crisis.

John C. Calhoun

To give added support to his demands, the President asked Congress for an authorization to use force in January of 1833. On February 20th, Congress passed the Force Bill, known as the

"Bloody Bill," which authorized Jackson to use military force in South Carolina. Jackson went beyond this, vowing to personally murder John C. Calhoun and "hang him high as Hamen." Such belligerent militance was typical of President Jackson, but Congress ultimately managed a compromise in March, authored by the "Great Compromiser" Henry Clay himself. The new bill reduced all tariffs for a ten year period and was signed into law on March 15th. South Carolina revoked its Ordinance of Nullification, though it nullified the Force Bill in the same act. Regardless, the Nullification Crisis was over.

Clay

Despite the attempt to settle the question with the Missouri Compromise, the young nation kept pushing further westward, and with that more territory was acquired. After the Mexican-American War ended in 1848, the sectional crisis was brewing like never before, with California and the newly-acquired Mexican territory now ready to be organized into states. The country was once again left trying to figure out how to do it without offsetting the slave-free state balance was tearing the nation apart.

With the new territory acquired in the Mexican-American War, pro and anti-slavery groups were at an impasse. The Whig Party, including a freshman Congressman named Abraham Lincoln, supported the Wilmot Proviso, which would have banned slavery in all territory acquired from Mexico, but the slave states would have none of it. Even after Texas was annexed as a slave state, the enormous new territory would doubtless contain many other new states, and the North hoped to limit slavery as much as possible in the new territories.

The Compromise of 1850 was authored by the legendary Whig politician Henry Clay. In addition to admitting California to the Union as a free state to balance with Texas, it allowed Utah and New Mexico to decide the issue of slavery on the basis of what became known as "popular sovereignty", which meant the settlers could vote on whether their state should be a free state or slave state. Though a Whig proposed popular sovereignty in 1850, popular sovereignty as an idea would come to be championed by and associated with Democratic Illinois Senator Stephen Douglas. The Compromise also abolished the slave trade – though not the existence of slavery itself – in Washington, D.C. The Whigs commended the Compromise, thinking it was a moderate, pragmatic proposal that did not decidedly extend the existence of slavery and put slow and steady limits on it. Furthermore, it made the preservation of the Union the top priority.

The Little Giant, Stephen Douglas

However, even though it added a new free state, many in the North were upset that the Compromise also included a new Fugitive Slave Act, which gave slaveholders increased powers to recapture slaves who had fled to free states by providing that a slave found in a free state could be ordered captured by police or federal marshals and returned to the slaveholder without any trial or due process whatsoever. In addition, no process was provided for the accused escaped slave to prove that he was actually free. This outraged most Northerners, who saw it as an unconstitutional infringement on the rights of their states and the rights of the individual accused of being an escaped slave. It also raised the specter of southern slave owners extending grip over the law enforcement of Northern states.

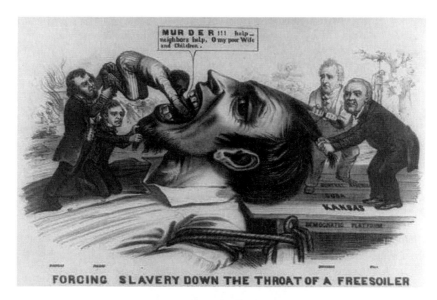

FORCING SLAVERY DOWN THE THROAT OF A FREESOILER

Some states even refused to comply. In Wisconsin, a rioting anti-slavery crowd freed an escaped slave who had been recaptured by federal marshals. When the leader of the riot was imprisoned, the Wisconsin Supreme Court held the Fugitive Slave Act unconstitutional. When the U.S. Supreme Court overturned that decision, the Wisconsin Legislature simply refused to comply with the Fugitive Slave Act or enforce it. Similarly, other Northern states passed laws restricting the ability of federal marshals or bounty hunters to recapture escaped slaves, and they also made it illegal for state officials to help recapture escaped slaves or use state jails for that purpose.

By 1853 and 1854, Henry Clay's Compromise of 1850 came under withering assault, because the Compromise had not settled all territory needed to be admitted for statehood. In an attempt to organize the center of North America – Kansas and Nebraska – without offsetting the slave-free balance, Senator Stephen Douglas of Illinois proposed the Kansas-Nebraska Act.

This proved to be the straw that broke the camel's back. First, the Kansas-Nebraska Act eliminated the Missouri Compromise line of 1820, which the Compromise of 1850 had maintained and had stipulated for over a generation that states north of the line would be free and states south of it *could* have slavery. This was essential to maintaining the balance of slave and free states in the Union. The Kansas-Nebraska Act, however, ignored the line completely and proposed that all new territories be organized by popular sovereignty. Settlers could vote whether they wanted their state to be slave or free.

When popular sovereignty became the standard in Kansas and Nebraska, the primary result was that thousands of zealous pro-slavery and anti-slavery advocates both moved to Kansas to influence the vote, creating a dangerous and ultimately deadly mix. Numerous attacks took place between the two sides, and many pro-slavery Missourians organized attacks on Kansas towns just across the border.

The most famous and infamous of them all was John Brown, perhaps the most controversial American of the 19th century. A radical abolitionist, Brown organized a small band of like-minded followers and fought with the armed groups of pro-slavery men in Kansas for several months, including a notorious incident known as the Pottawatomie Massacre, in which Brown's supporters murdered five men. Over 50 people died before John Brown left the territory, which ultimately entered the Union as a free state in 1859.

John Brown

While Brown acted militantly, politicians across the North, primarily Whigs and Free Soilers, were aghast over the Kansas-Nebraska Act. The suggestion that Congress could extend slavery into any unsettled territory violated some of their dearest held principles that slavery should not extend further. Whigs and Free Soilers in the North quickly coalesced against the "Slave Power", believing Southern influence in Washington had gone too far and now held the government in a strangle-hold. This coalescence first became known as the "anti-Nebraska" group, but it quickly vowed to form a new political party dedicated to keeping the Western territories free from slavery. They called themselves the Republicans.

Although destined to be forever associated with the Republican Party, Abraham Lincoln remained a Whig for some time. He agreed with the Republicans on the issue of Kansas-Nebraska, but he wasn't yet convinced that the Party of Clay was on its last legs. Instead, Lincoln focused his efforts on Stephen Douglas, the "Little Giant." The day after a major speech given by Douglas in which he defended his Kansas-Nebraska Act, Lincoln gave a speech known as the "Peoria Speech." On October 16th, 1854, Lincoln generated headlines with his speech, which laid out his opinion on slavery, a position he would keep only until the very last months of his Presidency.

"I wish to make and to keep the distinction between the existing institution, and the extension of it, so broad, and so clear, that no honest man can misunderstand me…

The doctrine of self government is right---absolutely and eternally right---but it has no just application, as here attempted. Or perhaps I should rather say that whether it has such just application depends upon whether a negro is not or is a man. If he is not a man, why in that case, he who is a man may, as a matter of self-government, do just as he pleases with him. But if the negro is a man, is it not to that extent, a total destruction of self-government, to say that he too shall not govern himself? When the white man governs himself that is self-government; but when he governs himself, and also governs another man, that is more than self-government---that is despotism. If the negro is a man, why then my ancient faith teaches me that 'all men are created equal;' and that there can be no moral right in connection with one man's making a slave of another.

Judge Douglas frequently, with bitter irony and sarcasm, paraphrases our argument by saying 'The white people of Nebraska are good enough to govern themselves, but they are not good enough to govern a few miserable negroes!!'

Well I doubt not that the people of Nebraska are, and will continue to be as good as the average of people elsewhere. I do not say the contrary. What I do say is, that no man is good enough to govern another man, without that other's consent. I say this is the leading principle---the sheet anchor of American republicanism. Our Declaration of Independence says:

'We hold these truths to be self evident: that all men are created equal; that they are endowed by their Creator with certain inalienable rights; that among these are life, liberty and the pursuit of happiness. That to secure these rights, governments are instituted among men, deriving their just powers from the consent of the governed.'

I have quoted so much at this time merely to show that according to our ancient faith, the just powers of governments are derived from the consent of the governed. Now the relation of masters and slaves is, PRO TANTO, a total violation of this principle. The master not only governs the slave without his consent; but he governs him by a set of rules altogether different from those which he prescribes for himself. Allow ALL the governed an equal voice in the government, and that, and that only is self government.

Let it not be said I am contending for the establishment of political and social equality between the whites and blacks. I have already said the contrary. I am not now combating the argument of NECESSITY, arising from the fact that the blacks are already amongst us; but I am combating what is set up as MORAL argument for allowing them to be taken where they have never yet been---arguing against the EXTENSION of a bad thing, which where it already exists, we must of necessity, manage as we best can."

Lincoln conceded the South's constitutional right to slavery in their states, but he firmly pushed back on the idea that it needed to be extended beyond where it already existed. Many Republicans anticipated slavery would die out on its own with time, and that this was the position of the Founders, meaning federal intervention was not needed to abolish slavery. However, they were bitterly opposed to popular sovereignty, which conceivably allowed slavery to be acceptable in any new state. Its extension - *anywhere* – was what Republicans wanted to disallow.

Dred Scott was an unlikely candidate to become the impetus and rallying cry of a brand new political party in the mid-19th century. Born into slavery in Virginia as Sam Scott, the young slave took the name of his older brother, Dred, after Dred's death, and he moved throughout Southern slave states as property of the Blow family until he was sold to U.S. Army doctor John Emerson in St. Louis, Missouri. Emerson's commission in the Army eventually brought him to the Wisconsin Territory in 1836, which was north of the line established by the Missouri Compromise of 1820 and was thus free territory where slavery was illegal. Naturally, Emerson brought his slaves along with him, and Dred Scott thus lived for an extended period of time in free territory, his slave status being a violation of the Missouri Compromise, the Northwest Ordinance, and the Wisconsin Enabling Act

By 1840, Dred Scott had married another slave of Emerson's named Harriet, and the couple had a child. Desperate to shake off the yoke of slavery but unable to buy his family's freedom, Scott sued for his freedom in Missouri, arguing that once he had entered free territory he could no longer be a slave. Scott's case made its way through the court system, and when the Missouri Supreme Court struck down a lower court ruling in Scott's favor, Scott and his lawyers appealed to the United States Supreme Court.

What followed was the 19th century's most important and far-reaching case, and probably its ugliest opinion. That year, a super-majority of seven Justices held that not only was Dred Scott a slave, but that he had no right to bring suit in the federal courts on any matter. In fact, the Court held that slaves could never be citizens and, as such, slaves and all persons of African descent lacked standing under Article III of the United States Constitution: "it is too clear for dispute, that the enslaved African race were not intended to be included, and formed no part of the people who framed and adopted this declaration. . . ." The Supreme Court also stated that persons of African descent "had no rights which the white man was bound to respect; and that the negro might justly and lawfully be reduced to slavery for his benefit. He was bought and sold and treated as an ordinary article of merchandise and traffic, whenever profit could be made by it." The Court invoked the Executive Branch's behavior and policy decisions to confirm what the operative phrase "citizen of the United States" meant.

Chief Justice Roger Taney

In short, a majority of the Supreme Court ruled that the Missouri Compromise of 1820, forbidding slavery in Northern territories, was unconstitutional as exceeding Congress's Article IV powers under the Property Clause ("The Congress shall have power to dispose of and make all needful Rules and Regulations respecting the Territory or other Property belonging to the United States; and nothing in this Constitution shall be so construed as to Prejudice any Claims of the United States, or of any particular State."). Therefore, although Scott had lived for a long period of time in Northern territories, he had never lawfully attained his freedom.

Taney hoped the case would help settle the growing political tension over the issue of slavery, but it had the opposite effect of becoming a springboard for Republicans and Abraham Lincoln. Much of the American public reacted virulently to the decision, fearing that this case would set a precedent for all slaves, and that slavery would spread unchecked. The Supreme Court did not predict this outcome; the Justices perhaps thought they were just bringing a sort of consensus to the issue by resolving it once and for all. Instead, every side of the issue only became more ardent in upholding or overturning the decision. The great abolitionist Frederick Douglass was despondent in *Dred Scott's* aftermath but also hopeful, stating that "my hopes were never brighter than now."

An 1860 political cartoon depicting Abraham Lincoln dancing with a black woman while Dred Scott plays the violin

The Republican Party, which was founded in 1854 primarily to stop the spread of slavery, was reinvigorated in their uphill battle to gain control of Congress and eventually the federal courts. Shortly after the decision, Lincoln commented about the case in a speech at Springfield on June 26, 1857, two weeks after Stephen Douglas had spoken there:

"And now as to the Dred Scott decision. That decision declares two propositions— first, that a Negro cannot sue in the U.S. Courts; and secondly, that Congress cannot prohibit slavery in the Territories. It was made by a divided court—dividing differently on the different points. Judge Douglas does not discuss the merits of the decision; and, in that respect, I shall follow his example, believing I could no more improve on McLean and Curtis, than he could on Taney.

He denounces all who question the correctness of that decision, as offering violent resistance to it. But who resists it? Who has, in spite of the decision, declared Dred Scott free, and resisted the authority of his master over him?

Judicial decisions have two uses—first, to absolutely determine the case decided, and secondly, to indicate to the public how other similar cases will be decided when they arise. For the latter use, they are called 'precedents' and 'authorities.'

We believe, as much as Judge Douglas, (perhaps more) in obedience to, and respect for the judicial department of government. We think its decisions on Constitutional questions, when fully settled, should control, not only the particular cases decided, but the general policy of the country, subject to be disturbed only by amendments of the Constitution as provided in that instrument itself. More than this would be revolution. But we think the Dred Scott decision is erroneous. We know the court that made it, has often over-ruled its own decisions, and we shall do what we can to have it to over-rule this. We offer no resistance to it.

I have said, in substance, that the Dred Scott decision was, in part, based on assumed historical facts which were not really true; and I ought not to leave the subject without giving some reasons for saying this; I therefore give an instance or two, which I think fully sustain me. Chief Justice Taney, in delivering the opinion of the majority of the Court, insists at great length that Negroes were no part of the people who made, or for whom was made, the Declaration of Independence, or the Constitution of the United States."

Of course, Lincoln's comments and thoughts about *Dred Scott* truly came to the fore during the Lincoln-Douglas debates. Throughout the fall of 1858, the two men participated in seven three-hour debates throughout Illinois. This unprecedented method of campaigning drew national attention, one that is still often idealized even today among those who feel politics is too bitterly partisan.

The main theme of the debates was the topic being discussed across the nation: slavery. When Congress created the territories of Kansas and Nebraska in 1854, it allowed the citizens of those territories to vote whether the new states would be free states or slave states. This idea of allowing the citizens to vote was known as "popular sovereignty", and it was championed by the Little Giant. Casting himself as a moderate, Douglas believed popular sovereignty would not divide the nation, and thinking further ahead he believed slavery could not thrive in the Western territories because the land there was inhospitable to slave labor anyway.

However, while Douglas viewed popular sovereignty as a more democratic means to solve problems, the North considered popular sovereignty a deliberate attempt to circumvent the Missouri Compromise, which was supposed to have banned slavery in any state above the parallel 36°30′ north. While Lincoln recognized the right of states to maintain slavery where it already existed, he strongly opposed the expansion of slavery and argued forcefully against popular sovereignty, which he thought threatened to expand slavery across the entire nation.

Douglas looked to blunt Lincoln's arguments during the debates by casting him as a radical

"Black Republican", accusing him of advocating for the social and legal equality of the races. Though he opposed slavery on moral grounds, Douglas also wanted to deny citizenship to all African-Americans, which the Supreme Court had ruled in the *Dred Scott* case. In his rebuttal, Lincoln offered one of his most quotable moments: "I protest against the counterfeit logic which concludes that, because I do not want a black woman for a slave, I must necessarily want her for a wife. I need not have her for either, I can just leave her alone."

Though Stephen Douglas was one of the most famous men of his time, and a far more famous and beloved figure than Lincoln when he died in 1861, today he has been remembered almost solely for his participation in the debates with the immortal Lincoln. With that, it has always been natural for Douglas to be portrayed as the antagonist in the story, and from a 21st century standpoint there's no question that his charges against Lincoln and the Black Republicans and his embrace of a white-supremacist platform cast him in a more negative light than Lincoln.

At the same time, some sympathizers have gone out of their way to argue that Douglas was personally opposed to slavery, but that he wouldn't let his personal views influence his stance on popular sovereignty. Civil War historian Allan Nevins has disputed that, arguing that when it came to Douglas, "When [slavery] paid it was good, and when it did not pay it was bad." In that same vein, historian Graham Peck points out that there is no evidence that can strongly prove Douglas was morally opposed to slavery, and that he was simply the "ideological, practical head of the northern opposition to the antislavery movement".

While nobody can deny that Lincoln hated slavery and worked to the utmost to prevent its spread, Lincoln was at his most forceful during the Lincoln-Douglas debates when responding to the accusation that he believed whites and blacks were equal, and that there should be racial equity in American society. It has long been convenient and politically expedient to separate Lincoln from his most controversial statements during the debates, which from a modern perspective must be viewed as nothing short of explicitly racist.

Of course, the Lincoln-Douglas debates have been sanitized in a similar vein. Today they are held out as an idealized example of a pure and civil, with two candidates politely delivering speeches and responses to each other without disruption or ad hominem attacks. They are remembered as good-natured, polite discourse, and they are held up as a gold standard by many in today's society who decry that national politics have become too partisan and too bitter, and that politics is now practiced in a world of instant sound bites. In high school debate halls across the country, and in debate societies, the Lincoln-Douglas debates have even lent their name to a particular kind of debate format, even though that format isn't the same as the one used by Stephen Douglas and Abraham Lincoln themselves.

Like the legacy of Abraham Lincoln himself, the popular perception of the Lincoln-Douglas has actually removed the elements of humanity from them. As the candidates' speeches and responses make clear, they were leveling charges that deeply offended each other, and responding by accusing each other of being liars. At times, Lincoln used his wit to devastating effect by humiliating Douglas with turns of phrase, in one debate claiming Douglas made a horse chestnut into a chestnut horse, and referring to the "Freeport Doctrine" as an idea that was "as thin as the homeopathic soup that was made by boiling the shadow of a pigeon that had starved to death." Far from being a different and purer kind of debate, the jokes were an 1858 variation of Ronald Reagan's "There you go again" quip in the 1980 debate against President Jimmy Carter. By the time they had debated each other a few times, Lincoln and Douglas could barely disguise their animosity toward one another.

The Lincoln-Douglas debates are rightly remembered as a forerunner to the nation's presidential debates, but they have taken on a legacy that does them disservice. Abraham Lincoln and Stephen Douglas were passionate advocates on two sides of the most critical political issues that ever faced the nation, and their words and arguments displayed that passion. Like their debates, Lincoln and Douglas were intelligent, important, and, most of all, human.

Chapter 2: A Political Speech

"Danville, Ill., Nov. 13, 1859.

James A. Briggs, Esq.,

Dear Sir: Yours of the 1st closing with my proposition for compromise, was duly received. I will be on hand; and in due time will notify you of the exact day. I believe, after all, I shall make a political speech of it. You have no objection? I would like to know, in advance, whether' I am also to speak or lecture in New York. Very, very glad your election went right.

Yours, truly,

A. Lincoln.

P. S. I am here at court, but my address is still at Springfield, 111."

By 1860, Lincoln had earned some renown during his 1858 race against the Little Giant, Stephen Douglas, for a U.S. Senate seat, but the arc of his political career changed on February 27 of that year when he spoke at the Cooper Institute in New York City. While the speech is today heralded as one of his finest moments, it's often forgotten how hard it was for the men in charge to even put the event together. According to James A. Briggs, who wrote about the event in 1915, "In October, 1859, Messrs. Joseph H. Richards, J. M. Pettingill, and S. W. Tubbs, called on me at the office of the Ohio State Agency, 25 William street, and requested me to write to the Hon. Thomas Corwin of Ohio, and the Hon. Abraham Lincoln of Illinois, and invite them to lecture, in a course of lectures these young gentlemen proposed for the winter, in Plymouth Church, Brooklyn. I wrote the letters as requested, and offered as compensation for each lecture, as I was authorized, the sum of Two hundred dollars. The proposition to lecture was accepted by

Messrs. Corwin and Lincoln. In due time Mr. Lincoln wrote me that he would deliver the lecture, a political one, on the evening of the twenty-seventh of February, 1860. This was rather late in the season for a lecture, and the young gentlemen who were' responsible were doubtful about its success, as the expenses were large. It was stipulated that the lecture was to be in Plymouth Church, Brooklyn; I requested and urged that the lecture should be delivered at the Cooper Institute. They were fearful it would not pay expenses — Three hundred and fifty dollars; — I thought it would. In order to relieve Messrs. Richards, Pettingill, and Tubbs, of all responsibility, I called upon some of the officers of the 'Young Men's Republican Union,' and proposed that they should take Mr. Lincoln, and that the lecture should be delivered under their auspices. They respectfully declined. I next called upon Mr. Simeon Draper, then President of 'The Draper Republican Union Club' of New York,' and proposed to him that his 'Union' take Mr. Lincoln and the lecture, and assume the responsibility of the expenses. Mr. Draper and his friends declined, and Mr. Lincoln was left in the hands of 'the original Jacobs.'" Needless to say, those who turned down the opportunity to meet and assist the future president would come to regret their decision.

Once it was decided who was sponsoring the event, those in charge had to act quickly to create a program that could successfully sell tickets. Briggs continued, "After considerable discussion, it was agreed on the part of the young gentlemen, that the lecture should be delivered in the Cooper Institute, if I would agree to share the expenses, if the sale of tickets (Twenty-five cents each) for the lecture did not meet the outlay. To this I assented — and the lecture was advertised to be delivered in the Cooper Institute, on the evening of the twenty seventh of February. Mr. Lincoln read the notice of the lecture in the papers, and, without any knowledge of the arrangement, was somewhat surprised to learn that he was first to make his appearance before a New York instead of a Plymouth Church audience. A notice of the proposed lecture appeared in the New York papers, and the Times spoke of him as a lawyer who had some local reputation in Illinois. At my personal solicitation, Mr. William Cullen Bryant presided as Chairman of the meeting, and introduced Mr. Lincoln for the first time to a New York audience."

Bryant

The local papers agreed that Briggs made a good choice in Lincoln; according to reports from the night, "The announcement that Hon. Abraham Lincoln of Illinois, would deliver an address in Cooper Institute, last evening, drew thither a large and enthusiastic assemblage. Soon after the appointed hour for commencing the proceedings, David Dudley Field, Esq., arose and nominated as Chairman of the meeting Mr. William Cullen Bryant. The nomination was received with prolonged applause, and was unanimously approved."

On that night, Bryant offered the following enthusiastic introduction of the tall lawyer from

Illinois: "It is a grateful office that I perform in introducing to you at this time an eminent citizen of the West, whom you know — whom you have known hitherto — only by fame, and who has consented to address a New York assemblage this evening. The great West, my friends, is a potent auxiliary in the battle we are fighting, for Freedom against Slavery; in behalf of civilization against barbarism; for the occupation of some of the fairest region of our Continent on which the settlers are now building their cabins. I see a higher and wiser agency than that of man in the causes that have filled with hardy people the vast and fertile regions which form the northern part of the valley of the Mississippi— a race of men who are not ashamed to till their acres with their own hands, and who would be ashamed to subsist on the labor of the slave. These children of the West, my friends, form a living bulwark against the advance of Slavery, and from them is recruited the vanguard of the armies of liberty. One of them will appear before you this evening in person — a gallant soldier of the political campaign of 1856 who then rendered good service to the Republican cause, and who has been since the great champion of that cause in the struggle which took place two years later for the supremacy of the Republicans in the Legislature of Illinois; who took the field against Senator Douglas, and would have won in the conflict but for the unjust provisions of the law of the State, which allowed a minority of the people to elect a majority of the Legislature. I have only, my friends, to pronounce the name of Abraham Lincoln of Illinois I have only to pronounce his name to secure your profoundest attention."

Although he received a warm applause, Lincoln's appearance still stunned at least one member of the audience, who later wrote, "When Lincoln rose to speak, I was greatly disappointed. He was tall, tall — oh, how tall! — and so angular and awkward that I had, for an instant, a feeling of pity for so ungainly a man. His clothes were black and ill-fitting, badly wrinkled — as if they had been jammed carelessly into a small trunk. His bushy head, with stiff black hair thrown back, was balanced on a long and lean head- stalk, and when he raised his hands in an opening gesture, I noticed that they were very large. He began in a low tone of voice — as if he were used to speaking outdoors, and was afraid of speaking too loud. He said, 'Mr. Cheerman,' instead of 'Mr. Chairman,' and employed many other words with an old-fashioned pronunciation. I said to myself: 'Old fellow, you won't do; it's all very well for the wild West, but this will never go down in New York.'"

Chapter 3: Great Authority

"I do not mean to say we are bound to follow implicitly in whatever our fathers did. To do so, would be to discard all the lights of current experience - to reject all progress - all improvement. What I do say is, that if we would supplant the opinions and policy of our fathers in any case, we should do so upon evidence so conclusive, and argument so clear, that even their great authority, fairly considered and weighed, cannot stand; and most surely not in a case whereof we ourselves declare they understood the question better than we." - Lincoln

Fittingly, as he approached the rostrum, Lincoln began his speech by referring to remarks made by his well-known nemesis, Senator Stephen Douglas.

"Mr. President and fellow citizens of New York:

The facts with which I shall deal this evening are mainly old and familiar; nor is there anything new in the general use I shall make of them. If there shall be any novelty, it will be in the mode of presenting the facts, and the inferences and observations following that presentation.

In his speech last autumn, at Columbus, Ohio, as reported in 'The New-York Times,' Senator Douglas said:

'Our fathers, when they framed the Government under which we live, understood this question just as well, and even better, than we do now.'

I fully indorse this, and I adopt it as a text for this discourse. I so adopt it because it furnishes a precise and an agreed starting point for a discussion between Republicans and that wing of the Democracy headed by Senator Douglas. It simply leaves the inquiry: 'What was the understanding those fathers had of the question mentioned?'"

Even today, people debate what the Founding Fathers intended in certain parts of the Constitution, but Lincoln took it a step further, asking, "What is the frame of government under which we live?" His answer was straightforward and set the boundaries in which his speech would be framed: "The answer must be: 'The Constitution of the United States.' That Constitution consists of the original, framed in 1787, (and under which the present government first went into operation,) and twelve subsequently framed amendments, the first ten of which were framed in 1789."

Lincoln them moved on to the next question, and the obvious answer to it: "Who were our fathers that framed the Constitution? I suppose the 'thirty-nine' who signed the original instrument may be fairly called our fathers who framed that part of the present Government. It is almost exactly true to say they framed it, and it is altogether true to say they fairly represented the opinion and sentiment of the whole nation at that time. Their names, being familiar to nearly all, and accessible to quite all, need not now be repeated. I take these 'thirty-nine,' for the present, as being 'our fathers who framed the Government under which we live.'"

By this time, those in the know could recognize a Socratic feel to the speech, or perhaps even something of the "call and response" spirit that influenced African-American worship. Lincoln continued, "What is the question which, according to the text, those fathers understood 'just as well, and even better than we do now?' It is this: Does the proper division of local from federal authority, or anything in the Constitution, forbid our Federal Government to control as to slavery in our Federal Territories? Upon this, Senator Douglas holds the affirmative, and Republicans the negative. This affirmation and denial form an issue; and this issue - this question - is precisely what the text declares our fathers understood 'better than we.'"

R.C. McCormick, who was in the audience that evening, later wrote, "Mr. Lincoln began his address at the Cooper Institute in a low, monotonous tone, but as he advanced, his quaint but clear voice rang out boldly and distinctly enough for all to hear. His manner was to a New York audience a very strange one, but it was captivating. He held the vast meeting spell-bound, and as one by one his oddly expressed but trenchant and convincing arguments confirmed the accuracy and irrefragability of his political conclusions, the house broke out in wild and prolonged enthusiasm. I think I never saw an audience more thoroughly earned away by an orator."

Ironically, Lincoln's effectiveness may have come as a result of his inability to read his own speech and the decision to go off the script. According to 19th century orator Russell H. Conwell, "Mr. Lincoln had in his hand a manuscript. He had written it with great care and exactness, and the speech which you read in his biography is the one that he wrote, not the one that he delivered as I recall it, and it is fortunate for the country that they did print the one that he wrote He had read three pages and had gone on to the fourth when he lost his place and then he began to tremble and stammer. He then turned it over two or three times, threw the manuscript upon the table, and, as they say in the West, 'let himself go.' Now the stammering man who had created only silent derision up to that point, suddenly flashed out into an angel of oratory and the awkward arms and disheveled hair were lost sight of entirely in the wonderful beauty and lofty inspiration of that magnificent address. The great audience immediately began to follow his thought, and when he uttered that quotation from (Frederick) Douglass, 'It is written in the sky of America that the slaves shall someday be free,' he had settled the question that he was to be the next President of the United States. The applause was so great that the building trembled and I felt the windows shake behind me."

Given that Lincoln deviated from his written speech and began to talk extemporaneously, it's impossible to know when or how he went off the script aside from some vague recollections made by those in attendance. As a result, the words in the speech are best remembered by the version later submitted to newspapers.

Regardless, the more Lincoln spoke, the more he warmed to his subject. According to Joseph Choate, a lawyer and diplomat, "When he spoke he was transformed, his eye kindled, his voice rang, his face shone and seemed to light up the whole assembly. For an hour and a half he held his audience in the hollow of his hand. His style of speech and manner of delivery were severely simple. What Lowell called 'the grand simplicities of the Bible,' with which he was so familiar, were reflected in his discourse."

The fact that Lincoln was from the West also had a pronounced effect on the crowd. 19th century journalist Ida M. Tarbell explained, "It is doubtful if there were any persons present, even his best friends, who expected that Lincoln would do more than interest his hearers by his sound arguments. Many have confessed since that they feared his queer manner and quaint speeches would amuse people so much that they would fail to catch the weight of his logic. But to the surprise of everybody Lincoln impressed his audience from the start by his dignity and his seriousness. 'His manner was, to a New York audience, a very strange one, but it was captivating,' wrote an auditor. 'He held the vast meeting spellbound, and as one by one his oddly expressed but trenchant and convincing arguments confirmed the soundness of his political conclusions, the house broke out in wild and prolonged enthusiasm. I think I never saw an audience more thoroughly carried away by an orator.'"

Chapter 4: Careful Preparation

"In the preceding October he came rushing into the office one morning with the letter from New York city inviting him to deliver a lecture there and asked ay advice and that of other friends as to the subject and character of his address. We all recommended a speech on the political situation. Remembering his poor success as a lecturer himself he adopted our suggestions. Ho accepted the invitation of the New York committee, at the same time notifying them that his speech would deal entirely with political questions, and fixing a day late in February as the most convenient I time. Meanwhile he spent the intervening time in careful preparation. He searched through the dusty volumes of congressional proceedings in the state library and dug deeply into political history. He was painstaking and thorough in the study of his subject, but when at last he left for New York we had many misgivings — and he not a few himself— of his success in the great metropolis. What effect the unpretentious western lawyer would have on the wealthy and fashionable society of the great city could only be conjectured." - William Herndon, Lincoln's law partner

Herndon

In the first part of his speech, Lincoln led his audience through a brief but comprehensive lesson in early American history, one that he knew many would be familiar with but few would have applied in the situation about which he was speaking. "Let us now inquire whether the 'thirty-nine,' or any of them, ever acted upon this question; and if they did, how they acted upon it - how they expressed that better understanding? In 1784, three years before the Constitution - the United States then owning the Northwestern Territory, and no other, the Congress of the Confederation had before them the question of prohibiting slavery in that Territory; and four of the 'thirty-nine' who afterward framed the Constitution, were in that Congress, and voted on that question. Of these, Roger Sherman, Thomas Mifflin, and Hugh Williamson voted for the prohibition, thus showing that, in their understanding, no line dividing local from federal authority, nor anything else, properly forbade the Federal Government to control as to slavery in federal territory. The other of the four - James McHenry - voted against the prohibition, showing that, for some cause, he thought it improper to vote for it. In 1787, still before the Constitution, but while the Convention was in session framing it, and while the Northwestern Territory still was the only territory owned by the United States, the same question of prohibiting slavery in the territory again came before the Congress of the Confederation; and two more of the 'thirty-nine' who afterward signed the Constitution, were in that Congress, and voted on the question. They were William Blount and William Few; and they both voted for the prohibition - thus showing that, in their understanding, no line dividing local from federal authority, nor anything else, properly forbids the Federal Government to control as to slavery in Federal territory. This time the prohibition became a law, being part of what is now well known as the Ordinance of '87."

Lincoln next went on to deal with one of the issues that haunts the nation to this day: the fact that men creating a government based on the idea that "all men are created equal" allowed slavery to not only exist but spread. Lincoln told the audience, "The question of federal control of slavery in the territories, seems not to have been directly before the Convention which framed the original Constitution; and hence it is not recorded that the 'thirty-nine,' or any of them, while engaged on that instrument, expressed any opinion on that precise question. In 1789, by the first Congress which sat under the Constitution, an act was passed to enforce the Ordinance of '87, including the prohibition of slavery in the Northwestern Territory. The bill for this act was reported by one of the 'thirty-nine,' Thomas Fitzsimmons, then a member of the House of Representatives from Pennsylvania. It went through all its stages without a word of opposition, and finally passed both branches without yeas and nays, which is equivalent to a unanimous passage. In this Congress there were sixteen of the thirty-nine fathers who framed the original Constitution. They were John Langdon, Nicholas Gilman, Wm. S. Johnson, Roger Sherman, Robert Morris, Thos. Fitzsimmons, William Few, Abraham Baldwin, Rufus King, William Paterson, George Clymer, Richard Bassett, George Read, Pierce Butler, Daniel Carroll, James Madison. This shows that, in their understanding, no line dividing local from federal authority, nor anything in the Constitution, properly forbade Congress to prohibit slavery in the federal territory; else both their fidelity to correct principle, and their oath to support the Constitution, would have constrained them to oppose the prohibition."

Lincoln then invoked the name dearest to 19th century Americans, and one that would have no rival in the country until after his own death. "Again, George Washington, another of the 'thirty-nine,' was then President of the United States, and, as such approved and signed the bill; thus completing its validity as a law, and thus showing that, in his understanding, no line dividing local from federal authority, nor anything in the Constitution, forbade the Federal Government, to control as to slavery in federal territory."

After discussing the country's revolutionary past, Lincoln moved on to the early 19th century. "No great while after the adoption of the original Constitution, North Carolina ceded to the Federal Government the country now constituting the State of Tennessee; and a few years later Georgia ceded that which now constitutes the States of Mississippi and Alabama. In both deeds of cession it was made a condition by the ceding States that the Federal Government should not prohibit slavery in the ceded territory. Besides this, slavery was then actually in the ceded country. Under these circumstances, Congress, on taking charge of these countries, did not absolutely prohibit slavery within them. But they did interfere with it - take control of it - even there, to a certain extent. In 1798, Congress organized the Territory of Mississippi. In the act of organization, they prohibited the bringing of slaves into the Territory, from any place without the United States, by fine, and giving freedom to slaves so brought. This act passed both branches of Congress without yeas and nays. In that Congress were three of the 'thirty-nine' who framed the original Constitution. They were John Langdon, George Read and Abraham Baldwin. They all, probably, voted for it. Certainly they would have placed their opposition to it upon record, if, in their understanding, any line dividing local from federal authority, or anything in the Constitution, properly forbade the Federal Government to control as to slavery in federal territory."

According to Lincoln's premise, everything changed when the western territories were acquired by the Louisiana Purchase. He also mentioned the primary topic on most Americans' minds: not whether slavery should continue where it was but whether it should be allowed to spread. Lincoln stated:

> "In 1803, the Federal Government purchased the Louisiana country. Our former territorial acquisitions came from certain of our own States; but this Louisiana country was acquired from a foreign nation. In 1804, Congress gave a territorial organization to that part of it which now constitutes the State of Louisiana. New Orleans, lying within that part, was an old and comparatively large city. There were other considerable towns and settlements, and slavery was extensively and thoroughly intermingled with the people. Congress did not, in the Territorial Act, prohibit slavery; but they did interfere with it - take control of it - in a more marked and extensive way than they did in the case of Mississippi. The substance of the provision therein made, in relation to slaves, was:

> First. That no slave should be imported into the territory from foreign parts.

> Second. That no slave should be carried into it who had been imported into the United States since the first day of May, 1798.

> Third. That no slave should be carried into it, except by the owner, and for his own use as a settler; the penalty in all the cases being a fine upon the violator of the law, and freedom to the slave.

> This act also was passed without yeas and nays. In the Congress which passed it, there were two of the 'thirty-nine.' They were Abraham Baldwin and Jonathan Dayton. As stated in the case of Mississippi, it is probable they both voted for it. They would not have allowed it to pass without recording their opposition to it, if, in their understanding, it violated either the line properly dividing local from federal authority, or any provision of the Constitution."

Lincoln then came to the Missouri Compromise: "In 1819-20, came and passed the Missouri question. Many votes were taken, by yeas and nays, in both branches of Congress, upon the various phases of the general question. Two of the 'thirty-nine' - Rufus King and Charles Pinckney - were members of that Congress. Mr. King steadily voted for slavery prohibition and against all compromises, while Mr. Pinckney as steadily voted against slavery prohibition and against all compromises. By this, Mr. King showed that, in his understanding, no line dividing local from federal authority, nor anything in the Constitution, was violated by Congress prohibiting slavery in federal territory; while Mr. Pinckney, by his votes, showed that, in his understanding, there was some sufficient reason for opposing such prohibition in that case."

At this point, Lincoln began to sum up his references to the original signers of the Constitution: "The cases I have mentioned are the only acts of the 'thirty-nine,' or of any of them, upon the direct issue, which I have been able to discover…To enumerate the persons who thus acted, as being four in 1784, two in 1787, seventeen in 1789, three in 1798, two in 1804, and two in 1819-20 - there would be thirty of them. But this would be counting John Langdon, Roger Sherman, William Few, Rufus King, and George Read each twice, and Abraham Baldwin, three times. The true number of those of the 'thirty-nine' whom I have shown to have acted upon the question, which, by the text, they understood better than we, is twenty-three, leaving sixteen not shown to have acted upon it in any way. Here, then, we have twenty-three out of our thirty-nine fathers 'who framed the government under which we live,' who have, upon their official responsibility and their corporal oaths, acted upon the very question which the text affirms they 'understood just as well, and even better than we do now;' and twenty-one of them - a clear majority of the whole 'thirty-nine' - so acting upon it as to make them guilty of gross political impropriety and willful perjury, if, in their understanding, any proper division between local and federal authority, or anything in the Constitution they had made themselves, and sworn to support, forbade the Federal Government to control as to slavery in the federal territories. Thus the twenty-one acted; and, as actions speak louder than words, so actions, under such responsibility, speak still louder."

Lincoln's words at this point in the speech revealed his genius, for while the country was divided on many issues of that present day, it remained united in its reverence for the Founding Fathers. By referring to them, he established a platform of agreement that everyone could all stand on together to discuss that things that were then dividing them. "Two of the twenty-three voted against Congressional prohibition of slavery in the federal territories, in the instances in which they acted upon the question. But for what reasons they so voted is not known. They may have done so because they thought a proper division of local from federal authority, or some provision or principle of the Constitution, stood in the way; or they may, without any such question, have voted against the prohibition, on what appeared to them to be sufficient grounds of expediency. No one who has sworn to support the Constitution can conscientiously vote for what he understands to be an unconstitutional measure, however expedient he may think it; but one may and ought to vote against a measure which he deems constitutional, if, at the same time, he deems it inexpedient. It, therefore, would be unsafe to set down even the two who voted against the prohibition, as having done so because, in their understanding, any proper division of local from federal authority, or anything in the Constitution, forbade the Federal Government to control as to slavery in federal territory. The remaining sixteen of the 'thirty-nine,' so far as I have discovered, have left no record of their understanding upon the direct question of federal control of slavery in the federal territories. But there is much reason to believe that their understanding upon that question would not have appeared different from that of their twenty-three compeers, had it been manifested at all. For the purpose of adhering rigidly to the text, I have purposely omitted whatever understanding may have been manifested by any person, however distinguished, other than the thirty-nine fathers who framed the original Constitution; and, for the same reason, I have also omitted whatever understanding may have been manifested by any of the 'thirty-nine' even, on any other phase of the general question of slavery. If we should look into their acts and declarations on those other phases, as the foreign slave trade, and the morality and policy of slavery generally, it would appear to us that on the direct question of federal control of slavery in federal territories, the sixteen, if they had acted at all, would probably have acted just as the twenty-three did. Among that sixteen were several of the most noted anti-slavery men of those times - as Dr. Franklin, Alexander Hamilton and Governor Morris - while there was not one now known to have been otherwise, unless it may be John Rutledge, of South Carolina. The sum of the whole is, that of our thirty-nine fathers who framed the original Constitution, twenty-one - a clear majority of the whole - certainly understood that no proper division of local from federal authority, nor any part of the Constitution, forbade the Federal Government to control slavery in the federal territories; while all the rest probably had the same understanding. Such, unquestionably, was the understanding of our fathers who framed the original Constitution; and the text affirms that they understood the question 'better than we.'"

One of the most stunning features of the speech was the breadth and depth of Lincoln's knowledge. When Nott and Brainerd published their copy of the Cooper Union Speech, they were forced to preface their work with the following admission: "No one who has not actually attempted to verify its details can understand the patient research and historical labor which it embodies. The history of our earlier politics is scattered through numerous journals, statutes, pamphlets and letters; and these are selective in completeness and accuracy of statement, and in indices and tables of contents. Neither can anyone who has not travelled over this precise ground appreciate the accuracy of every trivial detail, or the self-denying impartiality with which Mr. Lincoln has turned from the testimony of 'the fathers' on the general question of slavery to present the single question which he discusses. From the first line to the last — from his premises to his conclusion, he travels with a swift, unerring directness which no logician ever excelled— an argument complete and full, without the affectation of learning and without the stiffness which usually accompanies dates and details. A single, easy, simple sentence of plain Anglo-Saxon words contains a chapter of history that in some instances has taken days of labor to verify, and which must have cost the author months of investigation to acquire. And though the public should justly estimate the labor bestowed on the facts which are stated, they cannot estimate the greater labor involved on those which are omitted— how many pages have been read— how many works examined — what numerous statuses, resolutions, speeches, letters and biographies have been looked through. Commencing with this address, as a political pamphlet, the reader will leave it as an historical work— brief, complete, profound, impartial, truthful— which will survive the time and the occasion that called it forth, and be esteemed hereafter no less for its intrinsic worth than its unpretending modesty."

In the same vein, *The New York Evening Post* asserted, "The Cooper Institute address will live as one of the noblest productions of Mr. Lincoln's pen. It had much to do with securing for him the nomination at Chicago; indeed many are of the opinion that it was the single effort that made him the successful candidate in the convention. It's simple yet masterly style, its new and powerful logic, its mild and unanswerable disposition of the great agitating questions of the hour, its breadth and depth of spirit and tender sincerity, its lofty and eloquent patriotism, made it an appeal to the people alike opportune and forcible. It was circulated in many editions; by far the best being that supplied with copious and valuable notes by my friends Charles C. Nott and Cephas Brainerd, of this city. These gentlemen have often spoken to me of their surprise at the extensive reading; and research which Mr. Lincoln must have made serviceable in its preparation. Some of the works consulted by him they were weeks in finding."

The first section of Lincoln's speech was devastatingly effective because it disarmed some of the strongest arguments Southerners and popular sovereignty advocates like Stephen Douglas had previously put forward. As 19th Century journalist Ida Tarbell noted, "The Cooper Union speech was founded on a sentence from one of Douglas's Ohio speeches: 'Our fathers when they framed the government under which we live understood this question just as well, and even better, than we do now.' Douglas claimed that the 'fathers' held that the Constitution forbade the Federal government controlling slavery in the Territories. Lincoln, with infinite care, had investigated the opinions and votes of each of the 'fathers' — whom he took to be the thirty-nine men who signed the Constitution — and showed conclusively that a majority of them 'certainly understood that no proper division of local from Federal authority nor any part of the Constitution forbade the Federal government to control slavery in the Federal Territories.' Not only did he show this of the thirty-nine framers of the original Constitution, but he defied anybody to show that one of the seventy-six members of the Congress which framed the Constitution ever held any such view."

Having addressed the Declaration of Independence and the Founding Fathers, Lincoln's second part of the speech discussed current events, most notably *Dred Scott*. "But, so far, I have been considering the understanding of the question manifested by the framers of the original Constitution. In and by the original instrument, a mode was provided for amending it; and, as I have already stated, the present frame of 'the Government under which we live' consists of that original, and twelve amendatory articles framed and adopted since. Those who now insist that federal control of slavery in federal territories violates the Constitution, point us to the provisions which they suppose it thus violates; and, as I understand, that all fix upon provisions in these amendatory articles, and not in the original instrument. The Supreme Court, in the Dred Scott case, plant themselves upon the fifth amendment, which provides that no person shall be deprived of 'life, liberty or property without due process of law;' while Senator Douglas and his peculiar adherents plant themselves upon the tenth amendment, providing that 'the powers not delegated to the United States by the Constitution' 'are reserved to the States respectively, or to the people.' Now, it so happens that these amendments were framed by the first Congress which sat under the Constitution - the identical Congress which passed the act already mentioned, enforcing the prohibition of slavery in the Northwestern Territory. Not only was it the same Congress, but they were the identical, same individual men who, at the same session, and at the same time within the session, had under consideration, and in progress toward maturity, these Constitutional amendments, and this act prohibiting slavery in all the territory the nation then owned. The Constitutional amendments were introduced before, and passed after the act enforcing the Ordinance of '87; so that, during the whole pendency of the act to enforce the Ordinance, the Constitutional amendments were also pending."

Lincoln continued, "The seventy-six members of that Congress, including sixteen of the framers of the original Constitution, as before stated, were pre-eminently our fathers who framed that part of 'the Government under which we live,' which is now claimed as forbidding the Federal Government to control slavery in the federal territories. Is it not a little presumptuous in any one at this day to affirm that the two things which that Congress deliberately framed, and carried to maturity at the same time, are absolutely inconsistent with each other? And does not such affirmation become impudently absurd when coupled with the other affirmation from the same mouth, that those who did the two things, alleged to be inconsistent, understood whether they really were inconsistent better than we - better than he who affirms that they are inconsistent? It is surely safe to assume that the thirty-nine framers of the original Constitution, and the seventy-six members of the Congress which framed the amendments thereto, taken together, do certainly include those who may be fairly called 'our fathers who framed the Government under which we live.' And so assuming, I defy any man to show that any one of them ever, in his whole life, declared that, in his understanding, any proper division of local from federal authority, or any part of the Constitution, forbade the Federal Government to control as to slavery in the federal territories. I go a step further. I defy anyone to show that any living man in the whole world ever did, prior to the beginning of the present century, (and I might almost say prior to the beginning of the last half of the present century,) declare that, in his understanding, any proper division of local from federal authority, or any part of the Constitution, forbade the Federal Government to control as to slavery in the federal territories. To those who now so declare, I give, not only 'our fathers who framed the Government under which we live,' but with them all other living men within the century in which it was framed, among whom to search, and they shall not be able to find the evidence of a single man agreeing with them."

Following this last paragraph, McCormick noted that "the cheering was tumultuous," which naturally spurred Lincoln forward. "Now, and here, let me guard a little against being misunderstood. I do not mean to say we are bound to follow implicitly in whatever our fathers did. To do so, would be to discard all the lights of current experience - to reject all progress - all improvement. What I do say is, that if we would supplant the opinions and policy of our fathers in any case, we should do so upon evidence so conclusive, and argument so clear, that even their great authority, fairly considered and weighed, cannot stand; and most surely not in a case whereof we ourselves declare they understood the question better than we. If any man at this day sincerely believes that a proper division of local from federal authority, or any part of the Constitution, forbids the Federal Government to control as to slavery in the federal territories, he is right to say so, and to enforce his position by all truthful evidence and fair argument which he can. But he has no right to mislead others, who have less access to history, and less leisure to study it, into the false belief that 'our fathers who framed the Government under which we live' were of the same opinion - thus substituting falsehood and deception for truthful evidence and fair argument. If any man at this day sincerely believes 'our fathers who framed the Government under which we live,' used and applied principles, in other cases, which ought to have led them to understand that a proper division of local from federal authority or some part of the Constitution, forbids the Federal Government to control as to slavery in the federal territories, he is right to say so. But he should, at the same time, brave the responsibility of declaring that, in his opinion, he understands their principles better than they did themselves; and especially should he not shirk that responsibility by asserting that they 'understood the question just as well, and even better, than we do now.'"

By this time, the audience was thoroughly with him. Choate later observed, "With no attempt at ornament or rhetoric, without parade or pretense, he spoke straight to the point. If any came expecting the turgid eloquence of the ribaldry of the frontier they must have been startled at the earnest and sincere purity of his utterances. It was marvelous to see how this untutored man by mere self-discipline and the chastening of his own spirit, had outgrown all meretricious arts and found his way to the grandeur and strength of absolute simplicity. He spoke upon the theme which he had mastered so thoroughly. He demonstrated by copious historical proofs and masterly logic that the fathers who created the Constitution in order to form a more perfect union, to establish justice and to secure the blessings of liberty to themselves and their posterity, intended to empower the Federal Government to exclude slavery from the territories."

Before moving on to the second part of the speech, which addressed the South directly, Lincoln framed the Republican Party's interests in sum: "But enough! Let all who believe that 'our fathers, who framed the Government under which we live, understood this question just as well, and even better, than we do now,' speak as they spoke, and act as they acted upon it. This is all Republicans ask - all Republicans desire - in relation to slavery. As those fathers marked it, so let it be again marked, as an evil not to be extended, but to be tolerated and protected only because of and so far as its actual presence among us makes that toleration and protection a necessity. Let all the guarantees those fathers gave it, be, not grudgingly, but fully and fairly, maintained. For this Republicans contend, and with this, so far as I know or believe, they will be content."

Chapter 5: Inalienable Rights of Men

"I believe with you, that it is impossible for a people who are determined to perpetuate slavery at the expense of all the horrors of a civil war, to continue to hold slaves and live in peace with a government having its foundation on the equal and inalienable rights of men."- Peter Cooper, the founder of the Cooper Institute

Peter Cooper

Though it was unlikely that there were very many Southerners in his audience that night, Lincoln knew they would have the opportunity to read his words in the coming weeks. Thus, as Choate later wrote, "In the kindliest spirit he protested against the avowed threat of the Southern States to destroy the Union if, in order to secure freedom in those vast regions, out of which future States were to be carved, a Republican President were elected. He closed with an appeal to his audience, spoken with all the fire of his aroused and kindling conscience, with a full outpouring of his love of justice and liberty, to maintain their political purpose on that lofty and unassailable issue of right and wrong which alone could justify it and not to be intimidated from their high resolve and sacred duty by any threats of destruction to the Government or of ruin to themselves."

As Lincoln turned to the South directly, he began with these words: "And now, if they would listen - as I suppose they will not - I would address a few words to the Southern people. I would say to them: - You consider yourselves a reasonable and a just people; and I consider that in the general qualities of reason and justice you are not inferior to any other people. Still, when you speak of us Republicans, you do so only to denounce us a reptiles, or, at the best, as no better than outlaws. You will grant a hearing to pirates or murderers, but nothing like it to 'Black Republicans.' In all your contentions with one another, each of you deems an unconditional condemnation of 'Black Republicanism' as the first thing to be attended to. Indeed, such condemnation of us seems to be an indispensable prerequisite - license, so to speak - among you to be admitted or permitted to speak at all. Now, can you, or not, be prevailed upon to pause and to consider whether this is quite just to us, or even to yourselves? Bring forward your charges and specifications, and then be patient long enough to hear us deny or justify."

At this point, Lincoln used the politician's trick of pretending to speak to someone else in order to get one's own ideas across to an audience: "You say we are sectional. We deny it. That makes an issue; and the burden of proof is upon you. You produce your proof; and what is it? Why, that our party has no existence in your section - gets no votes in your section. The fact is substantially true; but does it prove the issue? If it does, then in case we should, without change of principle, begin to get votes in your section, we should thereby cease to be sectional. You cannot escape this conclusion; and yet, are you willing to abide by it? If you are, you will probably soon find that we have ceased to be sectional, for we shall get votes in your section this very year. You will then begin to discover, as the truth plainly is, that your proof does not touch the issue. The fact that we get no votes in your section, is a fact of your making, and not of ours. And if there be fault in that fact, that fault is primarily yours, and remains until you show that we repel you by some wrong principle or practice. If we do repel you by any wrong principle or practice, the fault is ours; but this brings you to where you ought to have started - to a discussion of the right or wrong of our principle. If our principle, put in practice, would wrong your section for the benefit of ours, or for any other object, then our principle, and we with it, are sectional, and are justly opposed and denounced as such. Meet us, then, on the question of whether our principle, put in practice, would wrong your section; and so meet it as if it were possible that something may be said on our side. Do you accept the challenge? No! Then you really believe that the principle which 'our fathers who framed the Government under which we live' thought so clearly right as to adopt it, and indorse it again and again, upon their official oaths, is in fact so clearly wrong as to demand your condemnation without a moment's consideration."

Lincoln slowly progressed from speaking to lecturing, castigating the South for its behavior up to that point and chiding those living there for misusing the words of Washington and others. "Some of you delight to flaunt in our faces the warning against sectional parties given by Washington in his Farewell Address. Less than eight years before Washington gave that warning, he had, as President of the United States, approved and signed an act of Congress, enforcing the prohibition of slavery in the Northwestern Territory, which act embodied the policy of the Government upon that subject up to and at the very moment he penned that warning; and about one year after he penned it, he wrote LaFayette that he considered that prohibition a wise measure, expressing in the same connection his hope that we should at some time have a confederacy of free States. Bearing this in mind, and seeing that sectionalism has since arisen upon this same subject, is that warning a weapon in your hands against us, or in our hands against you? Could Washington himself speak, would he cast the blame of that sectionalism upon us, who sustain his policy, or upon you who repudiate it? We respect that warning of Washington, and we commend it to you, together with his example pointing to the right application of it."

Lincoln continued challenging Southern leaders, questioning whether or not their values were as sincere and well-thought out as they could be. "But you say you are conservative - eminently conservative - while we are revolutionary, destructive, or something of the sort. What is conservatism? Is it not adherence to the old and tried, against the new and untried? We stick to, contend for, the identical old policy on the point in controversy which was adopted by 'our fathers who framed the Government under which we live;' while you with one accord reject, and scout, and spit upon that old policy, and insist upon substituting something new. True, you disagree among yourselves as to what that substitute shall be. You are divided on new propositions and plans, but you are unanimous in rejecting and denouncing the old policy of the fathers. Some of you are for reviving the foreign slave trade; some for a Congressional Slave-Code for the Territories; some for Congress forbidding the Territories to prohibit Slavery within their limits; some for maintaining Slavery in the Territories through the judiciary; some for the 'great principle' that 'if one man would enslave another, no third man should object,' fantastically called 'Popular Sovereignty;' but never a man among you is in favor of federal prohibition of slavery in federal territories, according to the practice of 'our fathers who framed the Government under which we live.' Not one of all your various plans can show a precedent or an advocate in the century within which our Government originated. Consider, then, whether your claim of conservatism for yourselves, and your charge or destructiveness against us, are based on the most clear and stable foundations. Again, you say we have made the slavery question more prominent than it formerly was. We deny it. We admit that it is more prominent, but we deny that we made it so. It was not we, but you, who discarded the old policy of the fathers. We resisted, and still resist, your innovation; and thence comes the greater prominence of the question. Would you have that question reduced to its former proportions? Go back to that old policy. What has been will be again, under the same conditions. If you would have the peace of the old times, readopt the precepts and policy of the old times."

As he saw the response he was getting from his audience, Lincoln went so far as to invoke the country's most controversial individual, John Brown, who had been hanged just two months earlier after his botched raid on Harper's Ferry. "You charge that we stir up insurrections among your slaves. We deny it; and what is your proof? Harper's Ferry! John Brown!! John Brown was no Republican; and you have failed to implicate a single Republican in his Harper's Ferry enterprise. If any member of our party is guilty in that matter, you know it or you do not know it. If you do know it, you are inexcusable for not designating the man and proving the fact. If you do not know it, you are inexcusable for asserting it, and especially for persisting in the assertion after you have tried and failed to make the proof. You need to be told that persisting in a charge which one does not know to be true, is simply malicious slander. Some of you admit that no Republican designedly aided or encouraged the Harper's Ferry affair, but still insist that our doctrines and declarations necessarily lead to such results. We do not believe it. We know we hold to no doctrine, and make no declaration, which were not held to and made by 'our fathers who framed the Government under which we live.' You never dealt fairly by us in relation to this affair. When it occurred, some important State elections were near at hand, and you were in evident glee with the belief that, by charging the blame upon us, you could get an advantage of us in those elections. The elections came, and your expectations were not quite fulfilled. Every Republican man knew that, as to himself at least, your charge was a slander, and he was not much inclined by it to cast his vote in your favor. Republican doctrines and declarations are accompanied with a continual protest against any interference whatever with your slaves, or with you about your slaves. Surely, this does not encourage them to revolt. True, we do, in common with 'our fathers, who framed the Government under which we live,' declare our belief that slavery is wrong; but the slaves do not hear us declare even this. For anything we say or do, the slaves would scarcely know there is a Republican party. I believe they would not, in fact, generally know it but for your misrepresentations of us, in their hearing. In your political contests among yourselves, each faction charges the other with sympathy with Black Republicanism; and then, to give point to the charge, defines Black Republicanism to simply be insurrection, blood and thunder among the slaves."

John Brown in 1859

With that, Lincoln maintained that the concerns of those in the South were unfounded, and that fears of a major slave rebellion or a federal attempt to abolish it were overblown: "Slave insurrections are no more common now than they were before the Republican party was organized. What induced the Southampton insurrection, twenty-eight years ago, in which, at least three times as many lives were lost as at Harper's Ferry? You can scarcely stretch your very elastic fancy to the conclusion that Southampton was 'got up by Black Republicanism.' In the present state of things in the United States, I do not think a general, or even a very extensive slave insurrection is possible. The indispensable concert of action cannot be attained. The slaves have no means of rapid communication; nor can incendiary freemen, black or white, supply it. The explosive materials are everywhere in parcels; but there neither are, nor can be supplied, the indispensable connecting trains. Much is said by Southern people about the affection of slaves for their masters and mistresses; and a part of it, at least, is true. A plot for an uprising could scarcely be devised and communicated to twenty individuals before some one of them, to save the life of a favorite master or mistress, would divulge it. This is the rule; and the slave revolution in Haiti was not an exception to it, but a case occurring under peculiar circumstances. The gunpowder plot of British history, though not connected with slaves, was more in point. In that case, only about twenty were admitted to the secret; and yet one of them, in his anxiety to save a friend, betrayed the plot to that friend, and, by consequence, averted the calamity. Occasional poisonings from the kitchen, and open or stealthy assassinations in the field, and local revolts extending to a score or so, will continue to occur as the natural results of slavery; but no general insurrection of slaves, as I think, can happen in this country for a long time. Whoever much fears, or much hopes for such an event, will be alike disappointed."

Determined to appeal to the patriotism of those in his audience and others who would later read his speech, Lincoln returned again to the ideas of the Founding Fathers. "In the language of Mr. Jefferson, uttered many years ago, 'It is still in our power to direct the process of emancipation, and deportation, peaceably, and in such slow degrees, as that the evil will wear off insensibly; and their places be, pari passu, filled up by free white laborers. If, on the contrary, it is left to force itself on, human nature must shudder at the prospect held up.' Mr. Jefferson did not mean to say, nor do I, that the power of emancipation is in the Federal Government. He spoke of Virginia; and, as to the power of emancipation, I speak of the slaveholding States only. The Federal Government, however, as we insist, has the power of restraining the extension of the institution - the power to insure that a slave insurrection shall never occur on any American soil which is now free from slavery."

Again, Lincoln returned to John Brown, determined to distance himself and the Republicans from the controversial abolitionist: "John Brown's effort was peculiar. It was not a slave insurrection. It was an attempt by white men to get up a revolt among slaves, in which the slaves refused to participate. In fact, it was so absurd that the slaves, with all their ignorance, saw plainly enough it could not succeed. That affair, in its philosophy, corresponds with the many attempts, related in history, at the assassination of kings and emperors. An enthusiast broods over the oppression of a people till he fancies himself commissioned by Heaven to liberate them. He ventures the attempt, which ends in little else than his own execution. Orsini's attempt on Louis Napoleon, and John Brown's attempt at Harper's Ferry were, in their philosophy, precisely the same. The eagerness to cast blame on old England in the one case, and on New England in the other, does not disprove the sameness of the two things. And how much would it avail you, if you could, by the use of John Brown, Helper's Book, and the like, break up the Republican organization? Human action can be modified to some extent, but human nature cannot be changed. There is a judgment and a feeling against slavery in this nation, which cast at least a million and a half of votes. You cannot destroy that judgment and feeling - that sentiment - by breaking up the political organization which rallies around it. You can scarcely scatter and disperse an army which has been formed into order in the face of your heaviest fire; but if you could, how much would you gain by forcing the sentiment which created it out of the peaceful channel of the ballot-box, into some other channel? What would that other channel probably be? Would the number of John Browns be lessened or enlarged by the operation?"

At this point, Lincoln began to phrase his arguments in terms of preserving the Union, a tactic that he would put to good use in the coming years. "But you will break up the Union rather than submit to a denial of your Constitutional rights. That has a somewhat reckless sound; but it would be palliated, if not fully justified, were we proposing, by the mere force of numbers, to deprive you of some right, plainly written down in the Constitution. But we are proposing no such thing. When you make these declarations, you have a specific and well-understood allusion to an assumed Constitutional right of yours, to take slaves into the federal territories, and to hold them there as property. But no such right is specifically written in the Constitution. That instrument is literally silent about any such right. We, on the contrary, deny that such a right has any existence in the Constitution, even by implication. Your purpose, then, plainly stated, is that you will destroy the Government, unless you be allowed to construe and enforce the Constitution as you please, on all points in dispute between you and us. You will rule or ruin in all events. This, plainly stated, is your language. Perhaps you will say the Supreme Court has decided the disputed Constitutional question in your favor. Not quite so. But waiving the lawyer's distinction between dictum and decision, the Court have decided the question for you in a sort of way. The Court have substantially said, it is your Constitutional right to take slaves into the federal territories, and to hold them there as property. When I say the decision was made in a sort of way, I mean it was made in a divided Court, by a bare majority of the Judges, and they not quite agreeing with one another in the reasons for making it; that it is so made as that its avowed supporters disagree with one another about its meaning, and that it was mainly based upon a mistaken statement of fact - the statement in the opinion that 'the right of property in a slave is distinctly and expressly affirmed in the Constitution.'"

The slaveholders of the South claimed that the Constitution enshrined the right to own slaves, but in opposing the spread of slavery in federal territories, Lincoln made his own arguments clear. "An inspection of the Constitution will show that the right of property in a slave is not distinctly and expressly affirmed in it. Bear in mind, the Judges do not pledge their judicial opinion that such right is impliedly affirmed in the Constitution; but they pledge their veracity that it is 'distinctly and expressly' affirmed there - 'distinctly,' that is, not mingled with anything else - 'expressly,' that is, in words meaning just that, without the aid of any inference, and susceptible of no other meaning. If they had only pledged their judicial opinion that such right is affirmed in the instrument by implication, it would be open to others to show that neither the word 'slave' nor 'slavery' is to be found in the Constitution, nor the word 'property' even, in any connection with language alluding to the things slave, or slavery; and that wherever in that instrument the slave is alluded to, he is called a 'person;' - and wherever his master's legal right in relation to him is alluded to, it is spoken of as 'service or labor which may be due,' - as a debt payable in service or labor. Also, it would be open to show, by contemporaneous history, that this mode of alluding to slaves and slavery, instead of speaking of them, was employed on purpose to exclude from the Constitution the idea that there could be property in man. To show all this, is easy and certain. When this obvious mistake of the Judges shall be brought to their notice, is it not reasonable to expect that they will withdraw the mistaken statement, and reconsider the conclusion based upon it? And then it is to be remembered that 'our fathers, who framed the Government under which we live' - the men who made the Constitution - decided this same Constitutional question in our favor, long ago - decided it without division among themselves, when making the decision; without division among themselves about the meaning of it after it was made, and, so far as any evidence is left, without basing it upon any mistaken statement of facts."

Finally, Lincoln concluded his remarks to Southerners: "Under all these circumstances, do you really feel yourselves justified to break up this Government unless such a court decision as yours is, shall be at once submitted to as a conclusive and final rule of political action? But you will not abide the election of a Republican president! In that supposed event, you say, you will destroy the Union; and then, you say, the great crime of having destroyed it will be upon us! That is cool. A highwayman holds a pistol to my ear, and mutters through his teeth, 'Stand and deliver, or I shall kill you, and then you will be a murderer!' To be sure, what the robber demanded of me - my money - was my own; and I had a clear right to keep it; but it was no more my own than my vote is my own; and the threat of death to me, to extort my money, and the threat of destruction to the Union, to extort my vote, can scarcely be distinguished in principle."

Chapter 6: Evidence of That Brain-Power

"It is now forty years since I first saw and heard Abraham Lincoln, but the impression which he left on my mind is inescapable. After his great success in the West he came to New York to make a political address. He appeared in every sense of the word like one of the plain people among whom he loved to be counted. At first sight there was nothing impressive or imposing about him, except that his great stature singled him out from the crowd; his clothes hung awkwardly on his giant frame; his face was of a dark pallor, without the slightest tinge of color; his seamed and rugged features bore the furrows of hardship and struggle; his deep set eyes looked sad and anxious: his countenance in repose gave little evidence of that brain-power which had raised him from the I lowest station among his countrymen." - Joseph Choate

In the final part of his speech, Lincoln turned his attention to his own supporters, following on the heels of the very moment when they were most delighted by his castigation of the South. "A few words now to Republicans. It is exceedingly desirable that all parts of this great Confederacy shall be at peace, and in harmony, one with another. Let us Republicans do our part to have it so. Even though much provoked, let us do nothing through passion and ill temper. Even though the southern people will not so much as listen to us, let us calmly consider their demands, and yield to them if, in our deliberate view of our duty, we possibly can. Judging by all they say and do, and by the subject and nature of their controversy with us, let us determine, if we can, what will satisfy them. Will they be satisfied if the Territories be unconditionally surrendered to them? We know they will not. In all their present complaints against us, the Territories are scarcely mentioned. Invasions and insurrections are the rage now. Will it satisfy them, if, in the future, we have nothing to do with invasions and insurrections? We know it will not. We so know, because we know we never had anything to do with invasions and insurrections; and yet this total abstaining does not exempt us from the charge and the denunciation. The question recurs, what will satisfy them? Simply this: We must not only let them alone, but we must somehow, convince them that we do let them alone. This, we know by experience, is no easy task. We have been so trying to convince them from the very beginning of our organization, but with no success. In all our platforms and speeches we have constantly protested our purpose to let them alone; but this has had no tendency to convince them. Alike unavailing to convince them, is the fact that they have never detected a man of us in any attempt to disturb them."

As he wound toward his conclusion, Lincoln threw himself into illustrating just how stubborn he considered Southerners to be: "These natural, and apparently adequate means all failing, what will convince them? This, and this only: cease to call slavery wrong, and join them in calling it right. And this must be done thoroughly - done in acts as well as in words. Silence will not be tolerated - we must place ourselves avowedly with them. Senator Douglas' new sedition law must be enacted and enforced, suppressing all declarations that slavery is wrong, whether made in politics, in presses, in pulpits, or in private. We must arrest and return their fugitive slaves with greedy pleasure. We must pull down our Free State constitutions. The whole atmosphere must be disinfected from all taint of opposition to slavery, before they will cease to believe that all their troubles proceed from us. I am quite aware they do not state their case precisely in this way. Most of them would probably say to us, 'Let us alone, do nothing to us, and say what you please about slavery.' But we do let them alone - have never disturbed them - so that, after all, it is what we say, which dissatisfies them. They will continue to accuse us of doing, until we cease saying. I am also aware they have not, as yet, in terms, demanded the overthrow of our Free-State Constitutions. Yet those Constitutions declare the wrong of slavery, with more solemn emphasis, than do all other sayings against it; and when all these other sayings shall have been silenced, the overthrow of these Constitutions will be demanded, and nothing be left to resist the demand. It is nothing to the contrary, that they do not demand the whole of this just now. Demanding what they do, and for the reason they do, they can voluntarily stop nowhere short of this consummation. Holding, as they do, that slavery is morally right, and socially elevating, they cannot cease to demand a full national recognition of it, as a legal right, and a social blessing."

With his final target revealed, Lincoln honed in on it with precision, demanding that his audience join him in abandoning all hypocrisy and looking at the world as it really was. "Nor can we justifiably withhold this, on any ground save our conviction that slavery is wrong. If slavery is right, all words, acts, laws, and constitutions against it, are themselves wrong, and should be silenced, and swept away. If it is right, we cannot justly object to its nationality - its universality; if it is wrong, they cannot justly insist upon its extension - its enlargement. All they ask, we could readily grant, if we thought slavery right; all we ask, they could as readily grant, if they thought it wrong. Their thinking it right, and our thinking it wrong, is the precise fact upon which depends the whole controversy. Thinking it right, as they do, they are not to blame for desiring its full recognition, as being right; but, thinking it wrong, as we do, can we yield to them? Can we cast our votes with their view, and against our own? In view of our moral, social, and political responsibilities, can we do this?"

With that, Lincoln finished his address: "Wrong as we think slavery is, we can yet afford to let it alone where it is, because that much is due to the necessity arising from its actual presence in the nation; but can we, while our votes will prevent it, allow it to spread into the National Territories, and to overrun us here in these Free States? If our sense of duty forbids this, then let us stand by our duty, fearlessly and effectively. Let us be diverted by none of those sophistical contrivances wherewith we are so industriously plied and belabored - contrivances such as groping for some middle ground between the right and the wrong, vain as the search for a man who should be neither a living man nor a dead man - such as a policy of "don't care" on a question about which all true men do care - such as Union appeals beseeching true Union men to yield to Disunionists, reversing the divine rule, and calling, not the sinners, but the righteous to repentance - such as invocations to Washington, imploring men to unsay what Washington said, and undo what Washington did. Neither let us be slandered from our duty by false accusations against us, nor frightened from it by menaces of destruction to the Government nor of dungeons to ourselves. LET US HAVE FAITH THAT RIGHT MAKES MIGHT, AND IN THAT FAITH, LET US, TO THE END, DARE TO DO OUR DUTY AS WE UNDERSTAND IT."

Chapter 7: Following the Cooper Institute Meeting

"The day following the Cooper Institute meeting the leading New York dailies published the speech in full and made favorable editorial mention of it and of the speaker as well. It was plain now that Lincoln had captured the metropolis. From New York he traveled to New England to visit his son Robert, who was attending college. In answer to the many calls and invitations which showered on him he spoke at various places in Connecticut, Rhode Island and New Hampshire. In all these places he not only left deep impressions of his ability, but he convinced New England of his intense earnestness in the great cause. The newspapers treated him with no little consideration. One paper characterized his speech as one of 'great-fairness,' delivered with 'great apparent candor and wonderful interest.' For the first half hour his opponents would agree with every word he uttered, and from that point he would lead them off little by little until it seemed as if he had got them all into his fold. He is far from prepossessing in personal appearance, and his voice is disagreeable, and yet he wins your attention from the start. He indulges in no flowers of rhetoric, no eloquent passages. He displays more shrewdness, more knowledge of the masses of mankind than any public speaker we have heard since Loup Jim Wilson left for California." - Herndon

By the time he was finished, Lincoln had made a profound impact on those who had thought lowly of him just 90 minutes earlier. The same audience member who had complained about Lincoln's "ungainly" appearance conceded, "[T]he whole man was transfigured. I forgot his clothes, his personal appearance, his individual peculiarities. Presently, forgetting myself, I was on my feet with the rest, yelling like a wild Indian, cheering this wonderful man. In the close parts of his argument, you could hear the gentle sizzling of the gas-burners. When he reached a climax the thunders of applause were terrific. It was a great speech. When I came out of the hall, my face glowing with excitement and my frame all aquiver, a friend with his eyes aglow, asked me what I thought of Abe Lincoln the rail-splitter. I said: 'He's the greatest man since St. Paul.' And I think so yet."

Choate closed his comments with a final observation of Lincoln's technique: "He concluded with this telling sentence, which drove the whole argument home to our hearts : 'Let us have faith that right makes might, and in that faith let us to the end dare to do our duty as we understand it.' "That night the great hall, and the nest day the whole city, rang with delighted applause and congratulations, and he who had come as a stranger departed with the laurels of a great triumph."

McCormick believed the address was something everybody in the crowd would remember for the rest of their lives. "Who that was present upon that occasion can forget it? A curiosity to see and hear the man who had dared 'To beard the lion in his den, The Douglass in his hall," rather than the expectation of an oratorical or literary least, had attracted a great audience. Upon the platform sat the Republican leaders of the city, and in the body of the hall there were many ladies. William Cullen Bryant, for whom Mr. Lincoln had during the day before expressed the highest admiration, took the chair, and introduced the speaker in a few graceful words…The language of Mr. Bryant, and the editorial of the Evening Post of the following day, expressing the wish that for the publication of such words of weight and wisdom as those uttered by Mr. Lincoln, the columns of that journal 'were indefinitely elastic,' were very pleasing to the 'eminent citizen of the West.'"

As the speech was published and quickly made its way into other papers around the country, it quickly vindicated those who had sponsored the event and put their faith in Lincoln. Briggs recalled with satisfaction, "The lecture was a wonderful success. It has become a part of the history of the country. Its remarkable ability was everywhere acknowledged; and after the twenty-seventh of February, the name of Mr. Lincoln was a familiar one to the people of the East. After Mr. Lincoln closed his lecture, Mr. David Dudley Field. Mr. James W. Nye, Mr. Horace Greeley, and myself, were called out by the audience, and made short speeches. I remember saying then: One of Three gentlemen will be our Standard Bearer in the Presidential contest of this year; the distinguished Senator of New York. Mr. Seward; the late able and accomplished Governor 'of Ohio, Mr. Chase; or the unknown knight who entered the political lists against the Bois Gilbert of Democracy, Stephen A. Douglas, on the prairies of Illinois in 1858, and unhorsed him — Abraham Lincoln. Some friends joked me after the meeting as not being a good prophet. The lecture was over; all the expenses were paid; I was handed by the gentlemen interested the sum of Four dollars and twenty-five cents as my share of the profits, as they would have called on me if there had been a deficiency in the receipts to meet expenses. Immediately after the lecture Mr. Lincoln went to Exeter, N. II., to visit his son Robert, then at school there, and I sent him a check for Two hundred dollars. Mr. Tubbs informed me a few weeks ago, that after the check was paid at the Park Bank he tore it up, but that he would give Two hundred dollars for the check if it could be restored — with the endorsement on it of A. Lincoln — as it was made payable to the order of Mr. Lincoln."

Briggs then relayed a most fitting anecdote: "After the return of Mr. Lincoln to New York from the East, where he had made several speeches, he said to me: 'I have seen what all the New York papers said about that thing of mine in the Cooper Institute, with the exception of the New York Evening Post, and I would like to know what Mr. Bryant thought of it;' and he then added: 'It is worth a visit from Springfield, Illinois, to New York, to make the acquaintance of such a man as William Cullen Bryant.' At Mr. Lincoln's request I sent him a copy of the Evening Post, with a. notice of his lecture. On returning from Mr. Beecher's church on a Sunday, in company with Mr. Lincoln, as we were passing the Post-office, I remarked to him: 'Mr. Lincoln, I wish you would take particular notice of what a dark and dismal place we have here for a Post-office, and I do it for this reason: I think your chance for being the next President is equal to that of any man in the country. When you are President will you recommend an appropriation of a million of dollars for a suitable location for a Post-office in this city?' With a significant gesture, Mr. Lincoln remarked, 'I will make a note of that.'"

A few months later, Lincoln became the Republican nominee essentially because of his moderate stance on slavery. Unlike many other viable Republican contenders, Lincoln was less likely to alienate valuable "battleground" states like Illinois, Indiana and Ohio. At the same time, the more staunchly abolitionist Northeast would have no better alternative.

Throughout the fall, the campaign broiled on. Presidential candidates in the mid-19th century did not campaign on their own behalf but let surrogates do the work for them, and supporters portrayed Lincoln as a man of great integrity from humble origins. Opponents conjured up the image of a radical Black Republican, which appealed well enough to the South that by the summer of 1860, talk of secession in the event of Lincoln's election was commonplace.

Lincoln in 1860

Indeed, the election of 1860 was held under extraordinary circumstances, and the results were equally unprecedented. Four candidates competed, and each of the candidates won some electoral votes. While the Republicans nominated Lincoln, the Democrats nominated Stephen Douglas, the Southern Democrats chose John C. Breckinridge, and the Constitutional Union Party selected John Bell of Tennessee. The Constitutional Union Party was compromised of former Know-Nothings and Whigs in the middle states of Kentucky, Tennessee and Virginia who advocated compromise and unity on the issue of slavery.

In fact, the race was so fractured that Lincoln only appeared on the ballot in five slave states: Virginia, Kentucky, Maryland, Delaware and Missouri. In Virginia, Lincoln only won about 1% of the vote, and in all the other slave states where Lincoln was on the ballot he finished no better than third. Lincoln won only two counties out all 996 counties in the 15 slave states.

On election night, Lincoln and the Republicans won decisively in the Electoral College, with 180 of the 303 votes cast and 152 needed for a majority. In the popular vote, Lincoln only garnered 39%, but he came out nearly half a million votes ahead of his next closest competitor, Stephen Douglas. In the Electoral College, Douglas only won 12 votes with a single state: Missouri. Lincoln swept the North, Breckinridge took the South, and Bell won most of the middle.

The results reflected the great regional divide, and the nation was set for Civil War.

Online Resources

The History of the Civil War: The Causes, Battles, and Generals of the War Between the States by Charles River Editors

Bibliography

Corry, John. *Lincoln at Cooper Union.* Xlibris. 2003.

Holzer, Harold. *Lincoln at Cooper Union: The Speech That Made Abraham Lincoln President.* Simon and Schuster. 2006.

Michael C. Leff and Gerald P. Mohrmann, "Lincoln at Cooper Union: A Rhetorical Analysis of the Text," rpt. in Readings in Rhetorical Criticism, 4th ed., Carl R. Burgchardt, Ed., State College, Pennsylvania: Strata, 2010, p. 166.

Perry, Bliss. Abraham Lincoln: early speeches, Springfield Speech, Cooper Union Speech, inaugural addresses, Gettysburg Address.... Amazon Digital Services, Inc. 2014.

The Gettysburg Address

Chapter 1: The Battle of Gettysburg

The Battle of Gettysburg is rightly remembered as being one of the Civil War's pivotal events, but it has taken on such a reputation as the war's biggest battle and crucial turning point that it is often viewed out of the context of the rest of the war. Regardless of whether some historians and others interested in the Civil War attach too much significance to it, Gettysburg was not fought in a vacuum, and the major battle that immediately preceded it had a great effect on some of the leading generals' decisions in Pennsylvania.

At the start of 1863, Confederate general Robert E. Lee had concluded an incredibly successful year for the Confederates in the East. Having taken command in June 1862, Lee led the Army of Northern Virginia to victory over George McClellan's Army of the Potomac in front of Richmond in the Peninsula Campaign, decisively defeated John Pope's Army of Virginia at the Second Battle of Bull Run, fought McClellan's Army of the Potomac to a tactical draw (but strategic defeat) in Maryland at Antietam, and inflicted a decisive defeat on Burnside's Army of the Potomac at Fredericksburg.

Lee

However, entering 1863 the Confederacy was still struggling. The Confederate forces in the West had failed to win a major battle, suffering defeat at places like Shiloh in Tennessee and across the Mississippi River. As the war continued into 1863, the southern economy continued to deteriorate. Southern armies were suffering serious deficiencies of nearly all supplies as the Union blockade continued to be effective as stopping most international commerce with the Confederacy. Moreover, the prospect of Great Britain or France recognizing the Confederacy had been all but eliminated by Lincoln issuing the Emancipation Proclamation in the wake of Antietam.

Given the unlikelihood of forcing the North's capitulation, the Confederacy's main hope for victory was to win some decisive victory or hope that Abraham Lincoln would lose his reelection bid in 1864, and that the new president would want to negotiate peace with the Confederacy. Understandably, this colored Confederate war strategy, and unquestionably Lee's.

In the spring of 1863, General Lee discovered that General George McClellan had known of his plans and was able to force a battle at Antietam in 1862 before all of General Lee's forces had arrived. General Lee now believed that he could successfully invade the North again, and that his defeat before was due in great measure to a stroke of bad luck. In addition, General Lee hoped to supply his army on the unscathed fields and towns of the North, while giving war ravaged northern Virginia a rest. After Chancellorsville, Corps commander James Longstreet and Lee met to discuss options for the Confederate Army's summer campaign. Longstreet advocated detachment of all or part of his corps to be sent to Tennessee, citing Union Maj. General Ulysses

S. Grant's advance on Vicksburg, the critical Confederate stronghold on the Mississippi River. Longstreet argued that a reinforced army under Bragg could defeat Rosecrans and drive toward the Ohio River, compelling Grant to release his hold on Vicksburg. Lee, however, was opposed to a division of his army and instead advocated a large-scale offensive (and raid) into Pennsylvania. In addition, General Lee hoped to supply his army on the unscathed fields and towns of the North, while giving war ravaged northern Virginia a rest.

Knowing that victories on Virginia soil meant little to an enemy that could simply retreat, regroup, and then return with more men and more advanced equipment, Lee set his sights on a Northern invasion, aiming to turn Northern opinion against the war and against President Lincoln. With his men already half-starved from dwindling provisions, Lee intended to confiscate food, horses, and equipment as they pushed north--and hopefully influence Northern politicians into giving up their support of the war by penetrating into Harrisburg or even Philadelphia. Given the right circumstances, Lee's army might even be able to capture either Baltimore or Philadelphia and use the city as leverage in peace negotiations.

After their victories at Fredericksburg and Chancellorsville against armies twice their size, Confederate troops felt invincible and anxious to carry the war north into Pennsylvania. As it turned out, the Confederates would blindly stumble into the Union Army of the Potomac outside of Gettysburg on July 1, 1863, and the first day of the battle by itself would have been one of the 25 biggest battles of the Civil War. The first day ended with a tactical Confederate victory, and Union casualties were almost 9,000, while the Confederates suffered slightly more than 6,000. But the battle had just started, and thanks to the actions of commander George Meade and one of his corps commanders, Winfield Scott Hancock, the largest battle on the North American continent would take place on the ground of their choosing.

On the morning of July 2, Meade was determined to make a stand at Gettysburg, and Lee was determined to strike at him. That morning, Lee decided to make strong attacks on both Union flanks while feinting in the middle, ordering Ewell's corps to attack Culp's Hill on the Union right while Longstreet's corps would attack on the Union left. Lee hoped to seize Cemetery Hill, which would give the Confederates the high ground to harass the Union supply lines and command the road to Washington, D.C. Lee also believed that the best way to do so would be to use Longstreet's corps to launch an attack up the Emmitsburg Road, which he figured would roll up the Union's left flank, presumed to be on Cemetery Hill. Lee was mistaken, due in part to the fact Jeb Stuart and his cavalry couldn't perform reconnaissance.

As it turned out, both attacks ordered by Lee would come too late. Though there was a controversy over when Lee ordered Longstreet's attack, Longstreet's march got tangled up and caused several hours of delay. Lost Cause advocates attacking Longstreet would later claim his attack was supposed to take place as early as possible, although no official Confederate orders gave a time for the attack. Lee gave the order for the attack around 11:00 a.m., and it is known that Longstreet was reluctant about making it; he still wanted to slide around the Union flank, interpose the Confederate army between Washington D.C. and the Army of the Potomac, and force Meade to attack them. Between Longstreet's delays and the mixup in the march that forced parts of his corps to double back and make a winding march, Longstreet's men weren't ready to attack until about 4:00 p.m.

Ultimately, it was the occupation and defense of Little Round Top that saved the rest of the Union line at Gettysburg. Had the Confederates commanded that high ground on the Union left, it would have been able to position artillery that could have swept the Union lines along Cemetery Ridge and Cemetery Hill, which would have certainly forced the Army of the Potomac to withdraw from their lines. The 20th Maine's Joshua L. Chamberlain would be awarded the coveted Congressional Medal of Honor for "daring heroism and great tenacity in holding his position on the Little Round Top against repeated assaults, and carrying the advance position on the Great Round Top", and the 20th Maine's actions that day became one of the most famous attacks of the Battle of Gettysburg and the Civil War as a whole.

Ewell's orders from Lee had been to launch a demonstration on the Union right flank during Longstreet's attack, which started at about 4:00 p.m. as well, and in support of the demonstration by Hill's corps in the center. For that reason, Ewell would not launch his general assault on Culp's Hill and Cemetery Hill until 7:00 p.m.

While the Army of the Potomac managed to desperately hold on the left, Ewell's attack against Culp's Hill on the other end of the field met with some success in pushing the Army of the Potomac back. However, the attack started so late in the day that nightfall made it impossible for the Confederates to capitalize on their success. Due to darkness, a Confederate brigade led by George H. Steuart was unaware that they were firmly beside the Army of the Potomac's right flank, which would have given them almost unlimited access to the Union army's rear and its supply lines and line of communication, just 600 yards away.

That night, Meade held another council of war. Having been attacked on both flanks, Meade and his top officers correctly surmised that Lee would attempt an attack on the center of the line the next day. Moreover, captured Confederates and the fighting and intelligence of Day 2 let it be known that the only Confederate unit that had not yet seen action during the fighting was George Pickett's division of Longstreet's corps.

Longstreet did not meet with Lee on the night of July 2, so when Lee met with him the following morning he found Longstreet's men were not ready to conduct an early morning attack, which Lee had wanted to attempt just as he was on the other side of the lines against Culp's Hill. With Pickett's men not up, however, Longstreet's corps couldn't make such an attack. Lee later wrote that Longstreet's "dispositions were not completed as early as was expected."

On the morning of July 3, the Confederate attack against Culp's Hill fizzled out, but by then Lee had already planned a massive attack on the Union center, combined with having Stuart's cavalry attack the Union army's lines in the rear. A successful attack would split the Army of the Potomac at the same time its communication and supply lines were severed by Stuart, which would make it possible to capture the entire army in detail.

There was just one problem with the plan, as Longstreet told Lee that morning: no 15,000 men who ever existed could successfully execute the attack. The charge required marching across an open field for about a mile, with the Union artillery holding high ground on all sides of the incoming Confederates. Longstreet ardently opposed the attack, but, already two days into the battle, Lee explained that because the Army of the Potomac was here on the field, he must strike at it. Longstreet later wrote that he said, "General Lee, I have been a soldier all my life. It is my opinion that no fifteen thousand men ever arrayed for battle can take that position." Longstreet proposed instead that their men should slip around the Union forces and occupy the high ground, forcing Northern commanders to attack them, rather than vice versa.

A picture of the field of Pickett's Charge taken from the Union Line near the High Water Mark. The ridge of trees is where the Confederate Line was positioned.

Realizing the insanity of sending 15,000 men hurtling into all the Union artillery, Lee planned to use the Confederate artillery to try to knock out the Union artillery ahead of time. Although old friend William Pendleton was the artillery chief, the artillery cannonade would be supervised by Porter Alexander, Longstreet's chief artillerist, who would have to give the go-ahead to the charging infantry because they were falling under Longstreet's command. Longstreet was certain of failure, but Pickett and the men preparing to make the charge were confident in their commanders and themselves.

Eventually, Union artillery chief Henry Hunt cleverly figured that if the Union cannons stopped firing back, the Confederates might think they successfully knocked out the Union batteries. On top of that, the Union would be preserving its ammunition for the impending charge that everyone now knew was coming. When they stopped, Lee, Alexander, and others mistakenly concluded that they'd knocked out the Union artillery.

A short time later, the Confederates were prepared to step out for the charge that bears Pickett's name, even though he commanded only about a third of the force and was officially under Longstreet's direction. Today historians typically refer to the charge as the Pickett-Pettigrew-Trimble Assault or Longstreet's Assault to be more technically correct. Since A.P. Hill was sidelined with illness, Pettigrew's and Trimble's divisions were delegated to Longstreet's authority as well. To make matters worse, Hill's sickness resulted in organizational snafus. Without Hill to assign or lead troops, some of his battle-weary soldiers of the previous two days were tapped to make the charge while fresh soldiers in his corps stayed behind.

Thus, about 15,000 Confederates stepped out in sight and began their charge with an orderly march starting about a mile away, no doubt an inspiring sight to Hancock and the Union men directly across from the oncoming assault. Pickett launched his attack as ordered, but within five minutes the men came to the top of a low rise where his line came into full view of Union defenses.

As the Confederate line advanced, Union cannon on Cemetery Ridge and Little Round Top began blasting away, with Confederate soldiers continuing to march forward. One Union soldier later wrote, "We could not help hitting them with every shot . . . a dozen men might be felled by one single bursting shell." By the time Longstreet's men reached Emmitsburg Road, Union artillery switched to firing grapeshot (tin cans filled with iron and lead balls), and as the Confederate troops continued to approach the Union center, Union troops positioned behind the wall cut down the oncoming Confederates, easily decimating both flanks. And while some of the men did manage to advance to the Union line and engage in hand-to-hand combat, it was of little consequence.

Today Pickett's Charge is remembered as the American version of the Charge of the Light Brigade, a heroic but completely futile march that had no chance of success. In fact, it's remembered as Pickett's Charge because Pickett's Virginians wanted to claim the glory of getting the furthest during the attack in the years after the war. The charge suffered about a 50% casualty rate while barely making a dent in the Union line before retreating in disorder back across the field. Pickett's post-battle report was apparently so bitter that Lee ordered it destroyed.

While nobody questions that Meade's strategy at Gettysburg was strong, he was heavily criticized by contemporaries for not pursuing Lee's army more aggressively as it retreated. Chief-of-staff Daniel Butterfield, who would call into question Meade's command decisions and courage at Gettysburg, accused Meade of not finishing off the weakened Lee. Meade would later state that as his army's new commander, he was uncertain of his troops' capabilities and strength, especially after a battle that had just resulted in over 20,000 Union casualties. Moreover, heavy rains made pursuit almost impossible on July 4, and Lee actually invited an attack during the retreat, hoping Meade would haphazardly attack strongly fortified positions.

Though historians now mostly credit Meade with making proper decisions in the wake of the battle, Lincoln was incredibly frustrated when Lee successfully retreated south. On July 14, Lincoln drafted a letter that he ultimately put away and decided not to send to Meade, who never read it during his lifetime:

"I have just seen your despatch to Gen. Halleck, asking to be relieved of your command, because of a supposed censure of mine. I am very--very--grateful to you for the magnificent success you gave the cause of the country at Gettysburg; and I am sorry now to be the author of the slightest pain to you. But I was in such deep distress myself that I could not restrain some expression of it. I had been oppressed nearly ever since the battles at Gettysburg, by what appeared to be evidences that yourself, and Gen. Couch, and Gen. Smith, were not seeking a collision with the enemy, but were trying to get him across the river without another battle. What these evidences were, if you please, I hope to tell you at some time, when we shall both feel better. The case, summarily stated is this. You fought and beat the enemy at Gettysburg; and, of course, to say the least, his loss was as great as yours. He retreated; and you did not, as it seemed to me, pressingly pursue him; but a flood in the river detained him, till, by slow degrees, you were again upon him. You had at least twenty thousand veteran troops directly with you, and as many more raw ones within supporting distance, all in addition to those who fought with you at Gettysburg; while it was not possible that he had received a single recruit; and yet you stood and let the flood run down, bridges be built, and the enemy move away at his leisure, without attacking him. And Couch and Smith! The latter left Carlisle in time, upon all ordinary calculation, to have aided you in the last battle at Gettysburg; but he did not arrive. At the end of more than ten days, I believe twelve, under constant urging, he reached Hagerstown from Carlisle, which is not an inch over fifty-five miles, if so much. And Couch's movement was very little different.

Again, my dear general, I do not believe you appreciate the magnitude of the misfortune involved in Lee's escape. He was within your easy grasp, and to have closed upon him would, in connection with our other late successes, have ended the war. As it is, the war will be prolonged indefinitely. If you could not safely attack Lee last Monday, how can you possibly do so South of the river, when you can take with you very few more than two thirds of the force you then had in hand? It would be unreasonable to expect, and I do not expect you can now effect much. Your golden opportunity is gone, and I am distressed immeasurably because of it.

I beg you will not consider this a prosecution, or persecution of yourself As you had learned that I was dissatisfied, I have thought it best to kindly tell you why."

Still, Meade was promoted to brigadier general in the regular army and was officially awarded the Thanks of Congress, which commended Meade "... and the officers and soldiers of [the Army of the Potomac], for the skill and heroic valor which at Gettysburg repulsed, defeated, and drove back, broken and dispirited, beyond the Rappahannock, the veteran army of the rebellion."

From almost the moment the Civil War ended, Gettysburg has been widely viewed as one of the decisive turning points of the Civil War. As renowned Civil War historian described Gettysburg, "It might be less of a victory than Mr. Lincoln had hoped for, but it was nevertheless a victory—and, because of that, it was no longer possible for the Confederacy to win the war. The North might still lose it, to be sure, if the soldiers or the people should lose heart, but outright defeat was no longer in the cards." While some still dispute that labeling, Lee's Army of Northern Virginia was never truly able to take the strategic offensive again for the duration of the war.

Naturally, if Gettysburg marked an important turning point in the Civil War, then to the defeated South it represented one of the last true opportunities the South had to win the war. After the South had lost the war, the importance of Gettysburg as one of the "high tide" marks of the Confederacy became apparent to everyone, making the battle all the more important in the years after it had been fought. Former Confederate comrades like Longstreet and Jubal Early would go on to argue who was responsible for the loss at Gettysburg (and thus the war) in the following decades. Much of the debate was fueled by those who wanted to protect Lee's legacy, especially because Lee was dead and could not defend himself in writing anymore. However, on July 3, Lee insisted on taking full blame for what occurred at Gettysburg, telling his retreating men, "It's all my fault." Historians have mostly agreed, placing the blame for the disastrous Day 3 on Lee's shoulders, and Porter Alexander would later call it Lee's "worst day" of the war.

However, after the war, former Confederates would not accept criticism of Lee, and blame for the loss at Gettysburg was thus placed upon other scapegoats. Although it was not immediately apparent where the blame rested for such a devastating loss, not long after the Battle of Gettysburg two names kept surfacing: cavalry leader General "Jeb" Stuart and General James

Longstreet; Stuart blamed for robbing Lee of the "eyes" he needed to know of Union movement, and Longstreet for delaying his attack on Round Top Hills the second day and acting too slowly in executing the assault on the Union left flank.

To a great extent, the Confederates' search for scapegoats is a product of the fact that they were so used to being successful that a defeat had to be explained by a Southern failure, not a Northern success. In casting about for Southern deficiencies, it is often overlooked that Meade and his top subordinates fought a remarkably efficient battle. Meade created an extremely sturdy defensive line anchored on high ground, he held the interior lines by having his army spread out over a smaller area, and he used that ability to shuffle troops from the right to the left on July 2. Moreover, Meade was able to rely on his corps commanders, especially Hancock, to properly use their discretion. Before the battle, Lee reportedly said that Meade "would commit no blunders on my front and if I make one ... will make haste to take advantage of it." If he said it, he was definitely right.

Perhaps none other than George Pickett himself put it best. When asked (certainly ad nauseam) why Pickett's Charge had failed, Pickett is said to have tersely replied, "I've always thought the Yankees had something to do with it."

Chapter 2: Planning a Dedication

"THE Battle of Gettysburg came to a close on the eve of Independence Day, 1863. The famous Gettysburg Address of Abraham Lincoln, however, was not made at the time of this important contest, and the remarks were not inspired by the militia in action. It was those brave men who had given 'the last full measure of devotion,' which drew from Lincoln the memorable words spoken on November 19, 1863, at the consecration of the Gettysburg National Cemetery. It was more than four months after the actual conflict that a part of the very field where men had fought was consecrated as a place where men were buried. The din and clamor of battle had given place to calm and quiet, and in an atmosphere charged with reverence and thoughts of the dead, the requiem pronounced by Abraham Lincoln was heard." - Louis A. Warren, *Little Known Facts About the Gettysburg Address*

In early November 1863, Abraham Lincoln received a letter that set in motion one of the defining moments of his presidency and American history as a whole. It had been written on November 2 by David Wills, who described himself as an "Agent for A.G. Curtin, Gov. of Penna. and acting for all the States." He wrote, "Sir, The Several States having Soldiers In the Army of the Potomac, who were killed at the battle of Gettysburg, or have since died at the various hospitals which were established in the vicinity, have procured grounds on a prominent part of the Battle Field for a Cemetery, and are having the dead removed to there and properly buried. These Grounds will be Consecrated and set apart to this sacred purpose, by appropriate Ceremonies on Thursday the 19th instant, - Hon Edward Everett will deliver the Oration. I am authorized by the Governors of the different States to invite you to be present, and participate in these ceremonies, which will doubtless be very imposing and solemnly impressive. It is the desire that, after the Oration, You, as Chief Executive of the Nation, formally set apart these grounds to their Sacred use by a few appropriate remarks. It will be a source of great gratification to the many widows and orphans that have been made almost friendless by the Great Battle here, to have you personally! and it will kindle anew in the breast of the comrades of these brave dead, who are now in the tented field or nobly meeting the foe in the front, a confidence that they who sleep in death on the Battle Field are not forgotten by those highest in authority; and they will feel that, should their fate be the same, their remains will not be uncared for. We hope you will be able to be present to perform this last solemn act to the Soldiers dead on the Battle Field."

Photograph of David Wills ca. 1856.

Wills

Governor Curtin

Edward Everett

It is difficult to guess what Lincoln must have felt when he received this letter. The Battle of Gettysburg, which had turned the tide of the Civil War in the Union's favor, had been a bloodbath, and while the casualty numbers are well-known, the cleanup of the area and the burial of soldiers over the coming weeks is often overlooked. The soldiers killed had been hastily buried immediately after the battle, often in unmarked mass graves, but not long after the battle ended, plans had been initiated to create a proper military cemetery on the site. According to an article carried in the *New York Tribune* in November 1863, "Soon after the memorable battle of Gettysburg, it occurred to the mind of David Wills, Esq., of this place, that if arrangements could be made for the purchase of a portion of the battle-field of Gettysburg for the purposes of a

'National Cemetery,' wherein should be placed the bodies of those of our men who fell in that battle, it would not only save a large expense in the removing of the bodies by the friends of the fallen brave, but would be something which, if rightly managed and carried out, we should all, as a nation, feel a just pride in. The idea was a good one ; for in what more appropriate place could those who so nobly fought and died for the institutions of their country and their perpetuation have than the spot where, struggling manfully and heartily, they chanced to fall? Mr. Wills, after much deliberation upon the matter, and after finding that his plan was at least feasible, had an interview with Gov. Curtin upon the subject. The Governor, who, throughout the State, is called the 'Soldier's Friend,' at once seized upon the idea, and after consultation with the Governors of the different States, ordered Mr. Wills to purchase, for the State of Pennsylvania, such ground as he might deem most suitable for the purpose. This was at once done, and some seventeen acres of land were purchased for the sum of $3,150; and arrangements were immediately made for the removing from the places where were so hastily buried after the battle, our brave Union defenders, and placing, within the grounds of the 'National Cemetery,' their hallowed remains."

By November, the stage was set to dedicate the new cemetery. The *Tribune* article continued, "From that time to the present this good work has been going on; and some six weeks since it had so far progressed as to fully prove its perfect success. It was then deemed advisable to appoint a day when the grounds so sacredly set apart should be formally consecrated with appropriate exercises. It should be mentioned here that each of the eighteen States represented at the battle, purchased portions of the grounds, and agreed with the Commonwealth of Pennsylvania that the future expense should be borne by each."

To commemorate this reburial, a special event to celebrate the Consecration of the National Cemetery at Gettysburg was planned for November 19, 1863, and Lincoln was asked to speak at it. Of course, he was not the only one, as the *Tribune* explained, "All things having thus been most satisfactorily arranged, Thursday, the 19th of this month, was fixed upon as the day of consecration; and Mr. Wills, whom Governor Curtin had previously appointed his agent, and who had also been specially selected by the other States to act for them all, through the newspapers of the land, invited all who so felt inclined, to lend their presence upon the occasion. It being considered a national undertaking, invitations were specially addressed to the Governors of all the loyal States, and various public men and notabilities."

John Nicolay, one of Lincoln's secretaries during the war, later noted, "Mr. Lincoln had a little more than two weeks in which to prepare the remarks he might intend to make. It was a time when he was extremely busy, not alone with the important and complicated military affairs in the various armies, but also with the consideration of his annual message to Congress, which was to meet early in December. There was even great uncertainty whether he could take enough time from his pressing official duties to go to Gettysburg at all. Up to the 17th of November, only two days before the ceremonies, no definite arrangements for the journey had been made."

Nicolay

Still, it seems that Lincoln was determined to go, writing to his Secretary of Treasury, Salmon P. Chase, on November 17: "I expected to see you here at cabinet meeting, and to say something about going to Gettysburg. There will be a train to take and return us. The time for starting is not yet fixed; but when it shall be I will notify you." By this time, Chase had already written to Wills declining to attend the ceremony, but in the meanwhile, the Secretary of War, Edwin Stanton, had written to Lincoln, "It is proposed by the Baltimore and Ohio road: First, to leave Washington Thursday morning at 6 A. M. Second, to leave Baltimore at 8 A. M., arriving at Gettysburg at twelve, noon, thus giving two hours to view the ground before the dedication ceremonies commence. Third, to leave Gettysburg at 6 P. M., and arrive at Washington at midnight, thus doing all in one day." Lincoln responded, "I do not like this arrangement. I do not wish to so go that by the slightest accident we fail entirely; and, at the best, the whole to be a mere breathless running of the gantlet. But any way."

Chapter 3: Writing the Speech

"IT WAS on November 2, seventeen days before the address, that the invitation to participate in the Gettysburg program reached Lincoln, and knowing his deep interest in the project, one would suggest that he immediately gave some thought to what he might say at the dedication. John Nicolay, one of his secretaries, observes that Lincoln 'probably followed his usual habit in such matters, using great deliberation in arranging his thoughts, and molding his phrases mentally, waiting to reduce them to writing until they had taken satisfactory form.' There is much difference of opinion as to when he found it convenient to write out his address, but all authorities in a position to know his movements in Washington are agreed that the first draft was written before he left the Capitol for Gettysburg. There is no dependable evidence, whatsoever, that indicates he wrote any part of the address on the way to Gettysburg. That some corrections in his manuscript were made after arriving at Gettysburg, and that the last part of it especially, was rewritten is an assured fact. The writing was done in the home of Mr. Wills where Lincoln was a guest. What is known as the battlefield revision copy is transcribed on two pieces of paper, the first part written in ink and the concluding part written in pencil." - Louis A. Warren, *Little Known Facts About the Gettysburg Address*

Since the speech itself is legendary, there are inevitably a bunch of legends concerning its composition, but at least some of the facts behind the speech's origins are understood. William H. Lambert, a well-known orator in his own right, wrote in 1909, "President Lincoln left Washington for Gettysburg at noon on Wednesday, November 18, 1863, in a special train consisting of four passenger coaches; he was accompanied by a large party that included members of his Cabinet, several foreign ministers, his private secretaries, officers of the Army and Navy, a military guard, and newspaper correspondents; the train arrived at Gettysburg about dark. Mr. Lincoln spent the night at the house of David Wills, Governor Curtin's representative and the active agent in the establishment of the Soldiers' Cemetery."

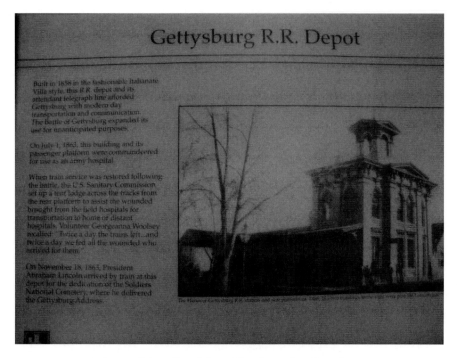

A picture of the railroad depot Lincoln used at Gettysburg

Aside from those facts, there is still an unsettled debate over some of the particulars. According to Isaac Arnold, who wrote, *History of Lincoln and the Overthrow of Slavery* in 1866, Lincoln "while on his way from the White House to the battlefield was notified that he would be expected to make some remarks," and "retiring to a seat by himself, with a pencil he wrote the address." 19th Century author Ben Perley Poore agreed, writing that "his remarks at Gettysburg…were written in the car on his way from Washington to the battlefield, upon a piece of pasteboard held on his knee."

While both these stories are charming, they are likely inaccurate; General James Fry, who was with Lincoln on the trip as an official escort, later wrote, "I have no recollection of seeing him writing or even reading his speech during the journey, in fact there was hardly any opportunity for him to read or write."

Years after the Civil War, Nicolay observed, "There is no decisive record of when Mr. Lincoln wrote the first sentences of his proposed address. He probably followed his usual habit in such matters, using great deliberation in arranging his thoughts, and molding his phrases mentally, waiting to reduce them to writing until they had taken satisfactory form. There was much greater necessity for such precaution in this case, because the invitation specified that the address of dedication should only be "a few appropriate remarks." Brevity in speech and writing was one of Lincoln's marked characteristics; but in this instance there existed two other motives calculated to strongly support his natural inclination. One was that Mr. Everett would be quite certain to make a long address; the other, the want of opportunity even to think leisurely about what he might desire to say. All this strongly confirms the correctness of the statement made by the Hon. James Speed, in an interview printed in the 'Louisville Commercial' in November, 1879, that the President told him that 'the day before he left Washington he found time to write about half of his speech.'"

William Mowry, author of *History of the United States for Schools* (1896), offered up Governor Curtin's description of events: "Governor Curtin said that after the arrival of the party from Washington, while the President and his Cabinet, Edward Everett, the orator of the day, Governor Curtin, and others were sitting in the parlor of the hotel, the President remarked that he understood that the committee expected him to say something. He would, therefore, if they would excuse him, retire to the next room and see if he could write out something. He was absent some time, and upon returning to the company had in his hand a large-sized, yellow government envelope. The President sat down, and remarked that he had written something, and with their permission he would like to read it to them, and invited them to criticize it. After reading what he had written upon the envelope, he asked for any suggestions they might make; Secretary Seward volunteered one or two comments, which Mr. Lincoln accepted and incorporated. Then he said, 'Now, gentlemen, if you will excuse me again, I will copy this off,' and returning again made a fresh copy to read from."

Seward

Judge Horatio King, who was also there that evening, told a slightly different story, claiming, "I saw Mr. Lincoln writing this address in Mr. Wills' house on a long yellow envelope. He may have written some of it before. He said 'I will go and show it to Seward,' who stopped at another house, which he did and then returned and copied his speech on a foolscap sheet."

On the other hand, Ward Lamon, a personal friend of Lincoln's, unequivocally insisted, "A day or two before the dedication of the National Cemetery at Gettysburg, Mr. Lincoln told me that he would be expected to make a speech on the occasion; that he was extremely busy, and had no time for preparation; and that he greatly feared he would not be able to acquit himself with credit, much less to fill the measure of public expectation. From his hat (the usual receptacle for his private notes and memoranda) he drew a sheet of foolscap, one side of which was closely written with what he informed me was a memorandum of his intended address. This he read to me, first remarking that it was not at all satisfactory to him. It proved to be in substance, if not in exact words, what was afterwards printed as his famous Gettysburg speech. … There is neither record, evidence, nor well-founded tradition that Mr. Lincoln did any writing, or made any notes, on the journey between Washington and Gettysburg. The train consisted of four passenger-coaches, and either composition or writing would have been extremely troublesome amid all the movement, the noise, the conversation, the greetings, and the questionings which ordinary courtesy required him to undergo in these surroundings ; but still worse would have been the rockings and joltings of the train, rendering writing virtually impossible. Mr. Lincoln carried in his pocket the autograph manuscript of so much of his address as he had written at Washington the day before. ... The whole of this first page — nineteen lines — is written in ink in the President's strong clear hand, without blot or erasure.... But when, at Gettysburg on the morning of the ceremonies, Mr. Lincoln finished his manuscript, he used a lead pencil, with which he crossed out the last three words of the first page, and wrote above them in pencil 'we here be dedica,' at which point he took up a new half sheet of paper — not white letter-paper as before, but a bluish- gray foolscap of large size with wide lines, habitually used by him for long or formal documents, and on this he wrote, all in pencil, the remainder of the word, and of the first draft."

There is another problem in trying to determine when exactly Lincoln wrote his famous speech. When he left Washington on the morning of November 18, he was coming down with what ended up being a case of smallpox. He began to notice that he wasn't feeling well that morning and mentioned an overall feeling of malaise to John Hay, one of his personal secretaries. The next morning, he confided in Nicolay that he was feeling unwell and a bit lightheaded. By the time the ceremony was over and he was back on the train, he was running a fever and complaining of a migraine headache. A few days later, he was diagnosed with smallpox, though fortunately only a mild case. Given how he was feeling, it would be all the more remarkable if Lincoln managed to craft a substantial portion of the speech despite feeling that poorly.

For his part, Lambert concluded, "Whatever revision may have been given to the Address en route to or at Gettysburg, whatever changes or additions may have been made in its delivery, the Address existed in substantially completed form before the President left Washington. There can be no doubt that he had given prolonged and earnest thought to the preparation of this Address; he had had more than two weeks' notice that he was desired to speak ; and although the demands upon his time and attention were such as to allow him little opportunity for uninterrupted thought, he appreciated the momentousness of the occasion, he knew how much was expected of him, and what was due to the honored dead, and he did not trust to the inspiration of the moment or rely upon his readiness as an impromptu speaker when he dedicated the Soldiers' Cemetery at Gettysburg, for he had wrought and re-wrought until there came into perfect form the noblest tribute to a cause and its heroes ever rendered by human lips."

Chapter 4: Lincoln in Gettysburg

"The Gettysburg program was arranged by the National Soldiers Cemetery Committee, and they selected Edward Everett as the orator for the occasion. The first date set for the exercises as Thursday, October 13, 1863, but Mr. Everett felt he could not be ready to speak so soon as that and then suggested that November 19 would be the earliest possible date on which he could appear. This date was approved. Officially, Lincoln had no voice in the plans for the celebration as it was not under the jurisdiction of the United States Government. Out of courtesy to him, however, in ample time to prepare the few remarks he was expected to make, he was invited by the committee in charge to participate in the ceremonies. This request he graciously accepted, apparently without any feeling that his invitation to be present was unduly belated, as is often alleged." - Louis A. Warren, *Little Known Facts About the Gettysburg Address*

Lincoln had only been informed of the proposed dedication ceremony 17 days before it actually took place, but he still had some influence over scheduling. According to Nicolay, "The President's criticism of the time-table first suggested must have struck Secretary Stanton as having force, for the arrangement was changed, so that instead of starting on Thursday morning, the day of the ceremonies, the President's special train left Washington at noon of Wednesday the 18th. Three members of the cabinet — Mr. Seward, Secretary of State, Mr. Usher, Secretary of the Interior, and Mr. Blair, Postmaster- General — accompanied the President, as did the French minister M. Mercier, the Italian minister M. Bertinatti, and several legation secretaries and attaches. Mr. Lincoln also had with him his private secretary Mr. Nicolay, and his assistant private secretary Colonel John Hay. Captain H. A. Wise of the navy and Mrs. Wise (daughter of Edward Everett) were also of the party; likewise a number of newspaper correspondents from Washington, and a military guard of honor to take part in the Gettysburg procession. Other parties of military officers joined the train on the way. No accident or delay occurred, and the party arrived in Gettysburg about nightfall."

When David Wills wrote to Lincoln that November, he enclosed a personal note that might seem amazing to modern readers in an era of heavy Secret Service details: "As the hotels in our town will be crowded and in confusion at the time referred to in the enclosed invitation, I write to invite you to stop with me. I hope you will feel it your duty to lay aside pressing business for a day to come on here to perform this last sad rite to our brave soldier dead, on the 19th inst. Governor Curtin and Hon. Edward Everett will be my guests at that time, and if you come you will please join them at my house."

A picture of the Wills letter to Lincoln

Lincoln took Wills up on his offer. As Nicolay later put it, "According to invitation Mr. Lincoln went to the house of Mr. Wills, while the members of the cabinet, and other distinguished persons of his party, were entertained elsewhere. Except during its days of battle the little town of Gettysburg had never been so full of people. After the usual supper hour the streets literally swarmed with visitors, and the stirring music of regimental bands and patriotic glee clubs sounded in many directions. With material so abundant, and enthusiasm so plentiful, a serenading party soon organized itself to call on prominent personages for impromptu speeches, and of course the President could not escape. The crowd persisted in calling him out, but Mr. Lincoln showed himself only long enough to utter the few commonplace excuses which politeness required."

Nicolay took it upon himself to record the president's words that day and later published them as having been the following: "I appear before you, fellow-citizens, merely to thank you for this compliment. The inference is a very fair one that you would hear me for a little while at least, were I to commence to make a speech. I do not appear before you for the purpose of doing so, and for several substantial reasons. The most substantial of these is that I have no speech to make. In my position it is somewhat important that I should not say any foolish things. [A voice: 'If you can help it.'] It very often happens that the only way to help it is to say nothing at all. Believing that is my present condition this evening, I must beg of you to excuse me from addressing you further."

The festivities continued into the evening and evolved into something of a political meeting. Nicolay reported, "The crowd followed the music to seek other notabilities, and had the satisfaction of hearing short speeches from Secretary Seward, Representatives McPherson and McKnight, Judge Shannon, Colonel John W. Forney, Wayne MacVeagh, and perhaps others. These addresses were not altogether perfunctory. A certain political tension existed throughout the entire war period, which rarely failed to color every word of a public speaker, and attune the ear of every public listener to subtle and oracular meanings. Even in this ceremonial gathering there was a keen watchfulness for any sign or omen which might disclose a drift in popular feeling, either on the local Pennsylvania quarrel between Cameron and Curtin, or the final success or failure of the Emancipation Proclamation; or whether the President would or would not succeed himself by a re-nomination and reelection in the coming campaign of 1864. There were still here and there ultra-radical newspapers that suspected and questioned Seward's hearty support of the emancipation policy. These made favorable note of his little address in which he predicted that the war would end in the removal of slavery, and that 'when that cause is removed, simply by the operation of abolishing it, as the origin and agent of the treason that is without justification and without parallel, we shall henceforth be united, be only one country, having only one hope, one ambition, and one destiny.'"

Finally, the group separated. Nicolay remembered, "Speech-making finally came to an end, and such of the visitors as were blessed with friends or good luck sought the retirement of their rooms, where in spite of brass-bands and glee- clubs, and the restless tramping of the less fortunate along the sidewalks, they slept the slumber of mental, added to physical, weariness."

The Wills House

The office in the Wills House

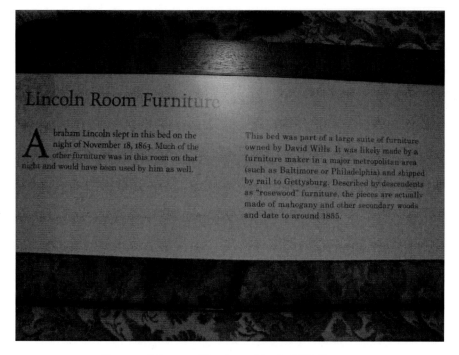

Lincoln Room Furniture

Abraham Lincoln slept in this bed on the night of November 18, 1863. Much of the other furniture was in this room on that night and would have been used by him as well.

This bed was part of a large suite of furniture owned by David Wills. It was likely made by a furniture maker in a major metropolitan area (such as Baltimore or Philadelphia) and shipped by rail to Gettysburg. Described by descendents as "rosewood" furniture, the pieces are actually made of mahogany and other secondary woods and date to around 1855.

Pictures of the room Lincoln used in the Wills House

Chapter 5: Delivering the Speech

"Gettysburg was an unlovely place on November 19, 1863. The trees, shorn of their limbs, gave evidence of the fearful struggle which had occurred there. The symmetry of the burial acres, with its semi-circular arrangement of lots, was entirely lost in the uneven newly made mounds with their crude markers. Interments were still being made as hastily prepared graves were being discovered from day to day. These physical surroundings contributed much to the solemnness of the gathering. The speakers' platform added little to the decorative features of the occasion. It was forty feet square and stood on the site now occupied by the Gettysburg National Monument. The platform faced away from the cemetery, however, so that the people assembled to hear the program would not be standing on that portion of the grounds where the soldiers were buried. The day itself, however, was a beautiful one and this contributed much to the comfort of the people. But the brightness of the sun only accentuated the ugliness of the place which is now so beautiful and serene." - Louis A. Warren, *Little Known Facts About the Gettysburg Address*

The next morning, the day dawned bright and clear, with just a nip of cold in the air. Lamon recalled, "It was after the breakfast hour on the morning of the 19th that the writer, Mr. Lincoln's private secretary, went to the upper room in the house of Mr. Wills which Mr. Lincoln occupied, to report for duty, and remained with the President while he finished writing the Gettysburg address, during the short leisure he could utilize for this purpose before being called to take his place in the procession, which was announced on the program to move promptly at ten o'clock."

The festivities began with a procession of important officials and dignitaries headed for the new cemetery, and perhaps the most definitive description of this was recorded by William Rathbone in 1938. During an oral history interview, he said, perhaps a bit idealistically, "Because, as a schoolboy, I was in the little town of Gettysburg in Pennsylvania some 75 years ago, I am privileged to tell you today what I then heard and saw when Abraham Lincoln, the wartime president of the United States, delivered his immortal address at the dedication of the national cemetery. When it was known that on a certain day in November, four months after the battle, that President Lincoln, 'Old Abe' as we boys affectionately called him, was to be in Gettysburg, I was excused from my duties at school and accompanied my family at least to see the president and perhaps to hear what he had to say. Bright and early the next morning, I was in the center square of the town where the procession was to form on the cemetery hill where the speaking was to take place. At the head of the procession, preceded by a mounted military band, the first I had ever seen, rode the president. He was mounted on a gray horse of medium size, which accentuated his unusual height, his long legs reaching too near the ground for either grace or good horsemanship. The president was escorted to the cemetery by many distinguished officers of the Army, representatives of foreign countries, military and civic organizations and the surging crowds of patriotic citizens estimated at 20,000."

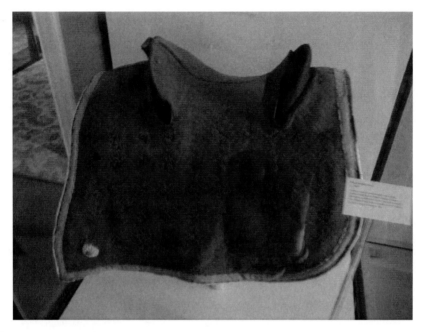

The saddle used by Lincoln to ride to the cemetery on November 19

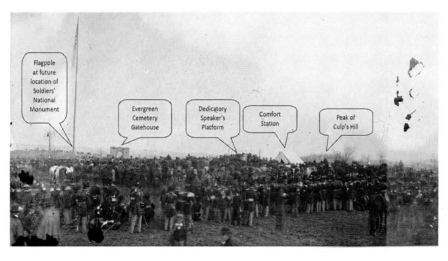

A picture of the crowd on November 19

Pictures of a Lincoln memorial in the cemetery

The program began with a rendition of "Homage d'uns Heroes" by Adolph Birgfeld that was performed by his own band. Then, the Reverend T. H. Stockton offered an Invocation. Next, the Marine Corp Band, under the direction of Francis Scala, performed a number, after which the Honorable Edward Everett stepped forward to give a nearly 13,000 word speech that lasted about two hours.

Everett's speech, entitled "The Battles of Gettysburg," was followed by the hymn "Consecration Chant," performed by the Baltimore Glee Club. It was only after all of these performances that Lincoln stepped forward for what were listed as "Dedicatory Remarks, by the President of the United States." By this time, according to Lambert, "The procession that had escorted the President to the field had been greatly belated, and after his arrival upon the platform the proceedings were still further delayed, awaiting the arrival of the orator of the day. Mr. Everett's oration, that had been preceded by a prayer of some length and by music, was of two hours' duration, so that when the President spoke it was to an audience that had been standing for nearly four hours. The brevity of the speech, the absence of rhetorical effort, and its very simplicity prevented its full appreciation."

According to the accepted record of the next two minutes, Lincoln made the following remarks, barely more than 250 words:

> "Four score and seven years ago our fathers brought forth on this continent a new nation, conceived in liberty, and dedicated to the proposition that all men are created equal.

> "Now we are engaged in a great civil war, testing whether that nation, or any nation so conceived and so dedicated, can long endure. We are met on a great battlefield of that war. We have come to dedicate a portion of that field, as a final resting place for those who here gave their lives that that nation might live. It is altogether fitting and proper that we should do this.

> "But, in a larger sense, we cannot dedicate, we cannot consecrate, we cannot hallow this ground. The brave men, living and dead, who struggled here, have consecrated it, far above our poor power to add or detract. The world will little note, nor long remember what we say here, but it can never forget what they did here. It is for us the living, rather, to be dedicated here to the unfinished work which they who fought here have thus far so nobly advanced. It is rather for us to be here dedicated to the great task remaining before us—that from these honored dead we take increased devotion to that cause for which they gave the last full measure of devotion—that we here highly resolve that these dead shall not have died in vain—that this nation, under God, shall have a new birth of freedom—and that government of the people, by the people, for the people, shall not perish from the earth."

Rathbone later remembered, "After the long, eloquent oration of Honorable Edward Everett of Massachusetts, conceded to be the most finished orator of his day, Lincoln arose and, with a manner serious almost to sadness, gave his brief address that rang from the hills of Gettysburg, around the world and back many times and will ever continue to reverberate in the hearts and minds of all mankind where freedom, forgiveness, tenderness and strength are cherished. During its delivery, with one or two other lads, I had worked my way onto the platform and wiggled through the crowd in front until I stood within 15 feet of Mr. Lincoln and looked up into his serious face. A rough board platform 4 or 5 feet high had been built from which the president spoke. Across the front, over the rail behind which he stood, was draped the nation's flag, the Stars and Stripes, Old Glory, as the soldiers gallantly called it. Although I listened intently to every word the president uttered and heard it clearly, boylike, I could not recall any of it afterwards. But had any of my companions spoken slightingly of it, there would have been a junior Battle of Gettysburg then and there, for any hint or intimation that Old Abe, as we affectionately called him, was deficient or delinquent in any respect would have meant a scrap, so deep-seated was our youthful loyalty."

Chapter 6: Reactions to the Speech

"Lincoln's words were few, two hundred and sixty-five, to be exact, according to the most dependable stenographic report. James Grant Wilson claims it took 'precisely one hundred and thirty-five seconds' to deliver the message. The President, a few days previous to leaving for Gettysburg had confided to a friend that his address was to be 'short — short — short.' The brevity of the message was not the most surprising characteristic of it, although it is said a photographer who planned to make a picture of Lincoln while speaking had insufficient time to get the camera adjusted before the address was over. The apparent care with which Lincoln had prepared the small part he was to take on the program was the outstanding feature of his efforts. As on occasions of similar dedications, according to Secretary Nicolay, the people were expecting 'a few perfunctory words, the mere formality of official dedication.' A formal statement by the President beginning, 'as President of the United States I hereby, etc.,' would have been appropriate but it was just like Lincoln to make something very beautiful out of a commonplace task. Without comment on what had been said before, without apology for lack of time, in simple and sympathetic words, he consecrated the burial field as 'a final resting place for those who here gave their lives.'" - Louis A. Warren, *Little Known Facts About the Gettysburg Address*

As Lambert astutely observed, part of the reason the history of the Gettysburg Address is still unsettled is the simple fact that it was recognized in hindsight as a masterpiece. As a result, negative perceptions at the time have been overlooked or completely forgotten, even by those who may have initially held such a view: "The Address has been so long and so generally accepted as the highest expression of American oratory, that it is difficult to realize that it ever had less appreciation than now. The testimonies of those who heard the Address delivered differ widely as to the reception given it and as to the impression it made."

For example, Clark Carr analyzed what he heard that day when he came to the battlefield cemetery from Illinois: "His expressions were so plain and homely, without any attempt at rhetorical periods, and his statements were so axiomatic, and, I may say, matter-of-fact, and so simple, that I had no idea that as an address it was anything more than ordinary. ... Everyone was impressed with his sincerity and earnestness.... There was one sentence that did deeply affect me — the only one in which the President manifested emotion. With the close of that sentence his lips quivered, and there was a tremor in his voice which I can never forget. ... The sentence was, ' The world will little note, nor long remember what we say here, but it can never forget what they did here"

Indeed, many people thought little of the Gettysburg Address in November 1863, including the president himself. Lamon, who stood with those listening to Lincoln that day, wrote of the speech, "After its delivery on the day of commemoration, [Lincoln] expressed deep regret that he had not prepared it with greater care. He said to me on the stand, immediately after concluding the speech: 'Lamon, that speech won't scour! It is a flat failure, and the people are disappointed.'

(The word 'scour' he often used in expressing his positive conviction that a thing lacked merit, or would not stand the test of close criticism or the wear of time.) He seemed deeply concerned about what the people might think of his address; more deeply, in fact, than I had ever seen him on any public occasion. His frank and regretful condemnation of his effort, and more especially his manner of expressing that regret, struck me as somewhat remarkable; and my own impression was deepened by the fact that the orator of the day, Mr. Everett, and Secretary Seward both coincided with Mr. Lincoln in his unfavorable view of its merits."

In analyzing Lincoln's opinion that his speech had not been well received, Lamon noted, "The occasion was solemn, impressive, and grandly historic. The people, it is true, stood apparently spell-bound; and the vast throng was hushed and awed into profound silence while Mr. Lincoln delivered his brief speech. But it seemed to him that this silence and attention to his words arose more from the solemnity of the ceremonies and the awful scenes which gave rise to them, than from anything he had said. He believed that the speech was a failure. He thought so at the time, and he never referred to it afterwards, in conversation with me, without some expression of unqualified regret that he had not made the speech better in every way. On the platform from which Mr. Lincoln delivered his address, and only a moment after it was concluded, Mr. Seward turned to Mr. Everett and asked him what he thought of the President's speech. Mr. Everett replied, 'It is not what I expected from him. I am disappointed.' Then in his turn Mr. Everett asked, 'What do you think of it, Mr. Seward?' The response was, 'He has made a failure, and I am sorry for it. His speech is not equal to him.' Mr. Seward then turned to me and asked, '…what do you think of it?' I answered, 'I am sorry to say that it does not impress me as one of his great speeches.'"

Lamon went on to clarify some of the rumors that had swirled about the speech in the years following its delivery: "In the face of these facts it has been repeatedly published that this speech was received by the audience with loud demonstrations of approval; that 'amid the tears, sobs, and cheers it produced in the excited throng, the orator of the day, Mr. Everett, turned to Mr. Lincoln, grasped his hand and exclaimed, 'I congratulate you on your success!' adding in a transport of heated enthusiasm, 'Ah, Mr. President, how gladly would I give my hundred pages to be the author of your twenty lines!'' Nothing of the kind occurred. It is a slander on Mr. Everett, an injustice to Mr. Lincoln, and a falsification of history. Mr. Everett could not have used the words attributed to him, in the face of his own condemnation of the speech uttered a moment before, without subjecting himself to the charge of being a toady and a hypocrite; and he was neither the one nor the other. As a matter of fact, the silence during the delivery of the speech, and the lack of hearty demonstrations of approval immediately after its close, were taken by Mr. Lincoln as certain proof that it was not well received. In that opinion we all shared. If any person then present saw, or thought he saw, the marvelous beauties of that wonderful speech, as intelligent men in all lands now see and acknowledge them, his superabundant caution closed his lips and stayed his pen. Mr. Lincoln said to me after our return to Washington, 'I tell you…that speech fell on the audience like a wet blanket. I am distressed about it. I ought to have prepared it with more care.' Such continued to be his opinion of that most wonderful of all his platform addresses up to the time of his death."

Lamon concluded his remarks on the subject with the following surprising evaluation: "I state it as a fact, and without fear of contradiction, that this famous Gettysburg speech was not regarded by the audience to whom it was addressed, or by the press and people of the United States, as a production of extraordinary merit, nor was it commented on as such until after the death of its author. Those who look thoughtfully into the history of the matter must own that Mr. Lincoln was, on that occasion, 'wiser than he knew.' He was wiser than his audience, wiser than the great scholars and orators who were associated with him in the events of that solemn day. He had unconsciously risen to a height above the level of even the 'cultured thought' of that period."

On the other hand, there were others present who immediately liked the speech. Congressman Robert Miller was present that day, and a few days later, he wrote, "The tall form of the President appeared on the stand and never before have I seen a crowd so vast and restless, after standing so long, so soon stilled and quieted. Hats were removed and all stood motionless to catch the first words he should utter, and as he slowly, clearly, and without the least sign of embarrassment read and spoke for ten minutes you could not mistake the feeling and sentiment of the vast multitude before him. I am convinced that the speech of the President has fully confirmed and I think will confirm all loyal men and women in the belief that Abraham Lincoln, though he may have made mistakes, is the right man in the right place."

Historian Samuel Bates considered what he heard that day unforgettable: "Its delivery was more solemn and impressive than is possible to conceive from its perusal. Major Harry T. Lee, who was one of the actors in the battle and who was present upon the platform at the dedication, says that the people listened with marked attention throughout the two hours that Mr. Everett spoke; …but that when Mr. Lincoln came forward and, with a voice burdened with emotion, uttered these sublime words the bosoms of that vast audience were lifted as a great wave of the sea ; and that when he came to the passage, ' The brave men living and dead, who struggled here,' there was not a dry eye."

Isaac Arnold agreed: "Before the first sentence was completed, a thrill of feeling like an electric shock pervaded the crowd. That mysterious influence called magnetism, which sometimes so affects a popular assembly, spread to every heart. The vast audience was instantly hushed and hung upon his every word and syllable. Everyone felt that it was not the honored dead only, but the living actor and speaker that the world for all time to come would note and remember, and that the speaker in the thrilling words he was uttering was linking his name forever with the glory of the dead… All his hearers realized that the great actor in the drama stood before them, and that the words he said would live as long as the language; that they were words which would be recollected in all future ages among all peoples, as often as men should be called upon to die for liberty and country. As he closed, and the tears and sobs and cheers which expressed the emotions of the people subsided, he turned to Everett and, grasping his hand, said, ' I congratulate you on your success.' The orator gratefully replied, 'Ah! Mr. President, how gladly would I exchange all my hundred pages to have been the author of your twenty lines.'"

Several decades later, Major Azor Nickerson, who was seated on the dais as Lincoln spoke, recalled, "Others, too, have differed as to the immediate effects of the President's remarks. I give the impressions received at the time, which were also identical with those of all with whom I spoke. I thought then and still think it was the shortest, grandest speech to which I ever listened. … My own emotions may perhaps be imagined when it is remembered that he was facing the spot where only a short time before we had our death grapple with Pickett's men and he stood almost immediately over the place where I had lain and seen my comrades torn in fragments by the enemy's cannon-balls — think then, if you please, how these words fell upon my ear. … If at that moment the Supreme Being had appeared with an offer to undo my past life, give back to me a sound body free from the remembrance even of sufferings past and the imminence of those that must necessarily embitter all the years to come, I should have indignantly spurned the offer, such was the effect upon me of this immortal dedication."

A committee of leading citizens from Boston reported back to their home town, "Perhaps nothing in the whole proceedings made so deep an impression on the vast assemblage or has conveyed to the country in so concise a form the lesson of the hour, as the remarks of the President, their simplicity and force make them worthy of a prominence among the utterances from high places."

Another man who heard the Gettysburg Address in person was Joseph L. Grant, a reporter for the Associated Press who wrote that there was "long, continual applause" at the close of the speech. Assuming that both Ward and Grant were telling the truth, the applause may have seemed to Lincoln and the others as only perfunctory, or maybe more in recognition of the occasion than the speech itself.

surrounded the position taken by the immense multitude of people.

The Marshal took up a position on the left of the stand. Numerous flags and banners, suitably draped, were exhibited on the stand among the audience. The entire scene was one of grandeur due to the importance of the occasion. So quiet were the people that every word uttered by the orator of the day must have been heard by them all, notwithstanding the immensity of the concours.

Among the distinguished persons on the platform were the following: Governors Bradford, of Maryland ; Curtin, of Pennsylvania ; Morton, of Indiana ; Seymour, of New-York ; Parker, of New-Jersey, and Tod, of Ohio ; Ex-Gov. Dennison, of Ohio ; John Brough, Governor Elect, of Ohio ; Charles Anderson, Lieutenant-Governor of Ohio ; Major-Generals Schenck, Stahel, Doubleday, and Couch ; Brigadier-General Gibbon ; and Provost-Marshal-General Fry.

PRESIDENT LINCOLN'S ADDRESS.

The President then delivered the following dedicatory speech :

Fourscore and seven years ago our Fathers brought forth upon this Continent a new nation, conceived in liberty and dedicated to the proposition that all men are created equal. [Applause.] Now we are engaged in a great civil war, testing whether that nation, or any nation so conceived and so dedicated, can long endure. We are met on a great battle-field of that war. We are met to dedicate a portion of it as the final resting-place of those who here gave their lives that that nation might live. It is altogether fitting and proper that we should do this. But in a larger sense we cannot dedicate. We cannot consecrate, we cannot hallow this ground. The brave men, living and dead, who struggled here have consecrated it far above our power to add or detract. [Applause.] The world will little note nor long remember, what we say here, but it can never forget what they did here. [Applause.] It is for us, the living, rather to be dedicated here to the refinished work that they have thus so far nobly carried on. [Applause.] It is rather for us to be here dedicated to the great task remaining before us, that from these honored dead we take increased devotion to that cause for which they here gave the last full measure of devotion ; that we here highly resolve that the dead shall not have died in vain ; [applause] that the Nation shall under God have a new birth of freedom, and that Governments of the people, by the people and for the people, shall not perish from the earth. [Long continued applause.]

Three cheers were then given for the President and the Governors of the States.

After the delivery of the addresses, the dirge and the benediction closed the exercises, and the immense assemblage separated at about 4 o'clock.

The *New York Times* report seems to match Grant's assessment of the applause

As is often the case, not everyone had the same recollection. John Russell Young, who also sat on the platform with Lincoln, remembered that reports claimed the speech "was studded with applause, but I do not remember the applause and am afraid the appreciative reporter was more than generous — may have put in the applause himself as a personal expression of opinion. ... I have read...of the emotions produced by the President's address, the transcendent awe that fell upon everyone who heard those most mighty and ever living words, to be remembered with pride through the ages, I have read of the tears that fell and the solemn hush, as though in a cathedral solemnity in the most holy moment of the Sacrifice. ... There was nothing of this, to the writer at least, in the Gettysburg Address."

While Lincoln's Gettysburg Address might not have made much of an impact on those who were not there, at least according to Lamon, is was a big hit in Europe. Lamon noted, "The marvelous perfection, the intrinsic excellence of the Gettysburg speech as a masterpiece of English composition, seem to have escaped the scrutiny of even the most scholarly critics of that day, on this side of the Atlantic. That discovery was made, it must be regretfully owned, by distinguished writers on the other side. The London 'Spectator,' the 'Saturday Review,' the 'Edinburgh Review,' and some other European journals were the first to discover, or at least to proclaim, the classical merits of the Gettysburg speech. It was then that we began to realize that it was indeed a masterpiece; and it dawned upon many minds that we had entertained an angel unawares, who had left us unappreciated."

The following day, one newspaper observed in an article entitled, "The Gettysburg Solemnities": "The proceedings at Gettysburg yesterday seem to have been, in every respect, appropriate. The presence of the President and many other distinguished men, together with a vast multitude of people from all parts of the country, shows how high is the popular estimate of the victory that was won by General Meade in July. It shows, too, how dearly the nation treasures the memories of the brave men who laid down their lives on those memorable days. Mr. Everett's oration is a fine, scholarly production. It is somewhat deficient in warmth, as is all that he writes; but it will serve as an enduring record, not merely of the dedication of the National Cemetery, but of the whole campaign which was crowned with victory at Gettysburg. The President's brief speech of dedication Is most happily expressed. It is warm, earnest, unaffected and touching. Thousands who would not read the long, elaborate oration of Mr. Everett will read the President's words, and not many of them will do it without a moistening of the eyes and a swelling of the heart. The really sacred soil of the battlefield of Gettysburg has now been solemnly set apart as the resting place of its heroes, and it will attract pilgrims from all parts of the land as long as we are a nation."

In a rare twist, that writer's prophetic words about both the speeches and the battlefield proved to be completely accurate.

Chapter 7: The Real Climax of All American Eloquence

"EDWARD EVERETT, principal speaker at the dedication, wrote to the President the day following the exercises and complimented him on the timeliness of his remarks. Everett said in part: 'Permit me also to express my great admiration of the thoughts expressed by you, with such eloquent simplicity and appropriateness, at the consecration of the Cemetery. I should be glad if I could flatter myself that I came as near the central idea of the occasion in two hours as you did in two minutes.' Lincoln's reply was as gracious as Mr. Everett's compliment. He wrote: 'I am pleased to know that in your judgment the little I did say was not entirely a failure. I knew Mr. Everett would not fail.' Mr. Everett did not fail in Lincoln's opinion, and more than a year later he was praising the words of Everett at Gettysburg. It is doubtful if Lincoln was ever conscious of the fact that his own Gettysburg Address was the real climax of all American eloquence." - Louis A. Warren, *Little Known Facts About the Gettysburg Address*

While Lincoln is famous for having been largely self-educated, he was a voracious reader with a keen mind, and after becoming more financially (and politically) successful, he had access to many of the classical works of literature. Therefore it is not surprising that he drew upon a number of sources to craft America's most famous speech.

For instance, historian Louis Warren noted similarities between the Gettysburg Address and Pericles' Funeral Oration during the Peloponnesian War as recounted by Thucydides. Warren explained, "Only one other great oration has been compared favorably with that of Lincoln at Gettysburg. That is the funeral oration by the immortal Pericles at Athens. There are many striking similarities in these two speeches. Both were delivered where brave men had fallen in battle. In Greece, Athenians had fought against Spartans, North against South, Greek against Greek. In America, the ground was where Puritan grappled with Cavalier, North faced the South, and American met American. Both Lincoln and Pericles began their orations with direct references to the contributions of the fathers.' Pericles began, 'I will begin then with our ancestors, our fathers inherited, etc.' Lincoln opened with, 'Four score and seven years ago, our fathers, etc.' It is significant that both orators, separated in time by centuries, should begin by commemorating the works of the fathers."

Then there was the issue of "government of the people, by the people, for the people." Warren noted, "Oft times a gem needs but the proper setting to bring out its brilliancy and full worth. Government of, by, and for the people was no new idea conceived by Abraham Lincoln, but he placed this jewel of democratic idealism as a crowning thought within the most eloquent oration of modern days. Five years before Gettysburg, Lincoln acquired two pamphlets containing addresses by Theodore Parker, delivered in 1858. In one of Parker's speeches, Lincoln underlined this statement: 'Democracy — The All Man Power; government over all, by all, and for the sake of all.' The other pamphlet contained a sermon delivered by Parker in Music Hall, Boston, on July 4, 1858, and these words Lincoln enclosed with a pencil: 'Democracy is Direct Self-Government over all the people, for all the people, by all the people.' Lincoln may have read in many instances statements which conveyed the thought with which he brought the Gettysburg Address to a close, but this slogan of a free people never had been spoken with more feeling, nor uttered in a more inspirational atmosphere, than on the nineteenth of November, 1863: 'That this nation, under God, shall have a new birth of freedom — and that government of the people, by the people, for the people, shall not perish from the earth.'"

Parker

In his evaluation of that particular phrase, Lamon wrote, "For using in his Gettysburg speech the celebrated phrase, 'the government of the people, by the people, and for the people,' Mr. Lincoln has been subjected to the most brutal criticism as well as to the most groundless flattery. Some have been base enough to insinuate against that great and sincere man that he was guilty of the crime of wilful plagiarism; others have ascribed to him the honor of originating the phrase entire. There is injustice to him in either view of the case. I personally know that Mr. Lincoln made no pretense of originality in the matter; nor was he, on the other hand, conscious of having appropriated the thought, or even the exact words, of any other man. If he is subject to the charge of plagiarism, so is the great Webster, who used substantially the same phrase in his celebrated reply to Hayne. Both men may have acquired the peculiar form of expression (the thought itself being as old as the republican idea of government) by the process known as unconscious appropriation. Certain it is that neither Lincoln nor Webster originated the phrase. Let us see how the case stands."

For his part, Lamon gave more credit to Parker: "In an address before the New England Antislavery Convention in Boston, May 29, 1850, Theodore Parker defined Democracy as 'a government of all the people, by all the people, for all the people, of course,' which language is identical with that employed by Mr. Lincoln in his Gettysburg speech. Substantially the same phrase was used by Judge Joel Parker in the Massachusetts Constitutional Convention in 1853. A distinguished diplomat has acquainted me with the singular fact that almost the identical phrase employed by Mr. Lincoln was used in another language by a person whose existence even was not probably known to Mr. Webster, the Parkers, or to Mr. Lincoln. On the thirty-first page of a work entitled 'Geschichte der Schweizerischen Regeneration von 1830 bis 1848, von P. Feddersen,' appears an account of a public meeting held at Olten, Switzerland, in May, 1830. On that occasion a speaker named Schinz used the following language, as translated by my friend just referred to: 'All the governments of Switzerland [referring to the cantons] must acknowledge that they are simply from all the people, by all the people, and for all the people. These extracts are enough to show that no American statesman or writer can lay claim to the origin or authorship of the phrase in question. No friend of Mr. Lincoln will pretend that it is the coinage of his fertile brain; nor will any fair-minded man censure him for using it as he did in his Gettysburg speech. As a phrase of singular compactness and force, it was employed by him, legitimately and properly, as a fitting conclusion to an address which the judgment of both hemispheres has declared will live as a model of classic oratory while free government shall continue to be known and revered among men."

William Herndon, Lincoln's partner in his Illinois law firm, also noted Parker's influence: "I brought with me additional sermons and lectures of Theodore Parker, who was warm in his commendation of Lincoln. One of these was a lecture on 'The Effect of Slavery on the American People' ... which I gave to Lincoln, who read and returned it. He liked especially the following expression, which he marked with a pencil, and which he in substance afterwards used in his Gettysburg Address: 'Democracy is direct self-government, over all the people, for all the people, by all the people.'"

Chief Justice John Marshall had written something similar decades earlier in the landmark case of *McCulloch v. Maryland* (1819): "The government of the Union, then (whatever may be the influence of this fact on the case), is, emphatically and truly, a government of the people. In form, and in substance, it emanates from them. Its powers are granted by them, and are to be exercised directly on them, and for their benefit."

As it turned out, the phrase pre-dated all of those men, for when John Wycliffe first translated the Bible into English in 1384, he prefaced his work with the statement, "This Bible is for the government of the people, for the people and by the people."

Another intriguing phrase in the address is "Under God." Warren observed, "ALL public speakers are aware that there comes to one spontaneously, on occasions of unusual emotional experiences, expressions which may have been lying dormant for years, apparently waiting for the proper moment to find voice. Lincoln's preliminary draft of the Gettysburg Address makes no mention of Deity, and this has been made a great point by those who would prefer to have it so. Every stenographic report of what Lincoln actually said, however, puts in the expression "under God" as having been spoken by the President. Back in Lincoln's childhood days, he had been greatly impressed by Weems' story of George Washington and he was able to quote many passages from this inspirational biography. Weems had one expression which he frequently used in his book, a word couplet — "under God." It was in the midst of Lincoln's final declaration that these two words sprang forth to hallow the entire address with the atmosphere of reverence."

The problem with the phrase "Under God" is that it did not appear any either of the first two drafts of his speech that Lincoln wrote before he gave it. However, it did appear in many of the published versions of the speech, including those taken from records made in short hand by stenographers during his address. Historian William Barton accepts that the stenographers were accurate in this case: "Every stenographic report, good, bad and indifferent, says 'that the nation shall, under God, have a new birth of freedom.' There was no common source from which all the reporters could have obtained those words but from Lincoln's own lips at the time of delivery. It will not do to say that [Secretary of War] Stanton suggested those words after Lincoln's return to Washington, for the words were telegraphed by at least three reporters on the afternoon of the delivery."

Lincoln also included it in later versions of the speech that he hand wrote at the request of others. Therefore, it seems most likely that, while it was not part of his original plan, he felt moved by the spirit of the moment to add the phrase while he was speaking. Ronald White, a professor religious history, asserted, "It was an uncharacteristically spontaneous revision for a speaker who did not trust extemporaneous speech. Lincoln had added impromptu words in several earlier speeches, but always offered a subsequent apology for the change. In this instance, he did not. And Lincoln included 'under God' in all three copies of the address he prepared at later dates. 'Under God' pointed backward and forward: back to 'this nation', which drew its breath from both political and religious sources, but also forward to a 'new birth'. Lincoln had come to see the Civil War as a ritual of purification. The old Union had to die. The old man had to die. Death became a transition to a new Union and a new humanity."

Chapter 8: Different Versions

"Five different versions of the Gettysburg address, strange to say, were all written or spoken by Abraham Lincoln, and there may have been others equally authentic. They can be identified as (1) preliminary writings, (2) spoken words, and (3) revisory copies. One author has put it like this, 'What he intended to say, what he said, what he wished he had said.' It is apparent that one copy of the address, and this one is also revised, by the way, was written preliminary to the delivery of the speech. There is no way of learning how many revisions the speech underwent before it finally was delivered. The most dependable record of what Lincoln actually said seems to have been made by a member of the Boston commission who went to Gettysburg, instructed to take down in shorthand the words of the President. This he did and his transcription was not jumbled by telegraph operators or rapid fire typesetters but was carefully and accurately prepared to be included in the commissioner's report. After the dedication, copies of Lincoln's address were requested by Edward Everett, George Bancroft, and probably others. The writing which he prepared for Everett and the two copies he wrote for Bancroft have been preserved. It is the version in the final Bancroft copy that is most widely used, and it has become known as the authentic Gettysburg Address of Abraham Lincoln." - Louis A. Warren, *Little Known Facts About the Gettysburg Address*

One of the things that makes analyzing the Gettysburg Address so challenging is that fact that there are at least five known versions of Lincoln's famous remarks, each with its own variations, critics and defenders. The first of these is the Nicolay Manuscript, considered by many to be the first draft of the speech, but over the next several decades, controversy raged over which manuscript matched the actual speech given at Gettysburg in November 1863. In 1909, the *Washington Star* reported, "That has been a matter of friendly controversy among interested parties almost from the day of its delivery. Among those who took part in this discussion were John Hay, former secretary of state, and John G. Nicolay, both of whom were secretaries to President Lincoln; Robert T. Lincoln, his surviving son; J. P. Nicholson, chairman of the Gettysburg National Military Park Commission; Gen. Aleshire, quarter master general; Gen. Oliver, assistant secretary of war, and many others. From the mass of correspondence on the subject it appears that there are three sources of authority for Lincoln's Gettysburg address, or rather three versions of it. They are all identical in thought, but differ slightly in expression."

For his part, Nicolay described the three versions mentioned as follows:

"1. The original autograph MS.[manuscript] draft, written by Mr. Lincoln partly at Washington and partly at Gettysburg. [Nicolay]

2. The version made by the shorthand reporter on the stand at Gettysburg when the President delivered It. which was telegraphed and was printed in the leading newspapers of the country on the following morning.

3. The revised copy made by the President a few days after his return to Washington, upon a careful comparison of his original draft and the printed newspaper version, with his own recollection of the exact form in which he delivered it." [Hay]

According to Lambert, "Nicolay says that the President did not read from the written pages, and that he did not deliver the Address in the form in which it was first written, but from the fulness of thought and memory rounded it out nearly to its final rhetorical completeness. Brooks states that as Mr. Lincoln read from the manuscript he made a few verbal changes. Comparison of the several reports named leads to the conclusion that the President, remembering what he had written in the Hay manuscript, delivered his Address in closer accordance with it than with the Nicolay manuscript which he held, but to which he referred little. The North American report, which in my judgment reproduces the words spoken more accurately than any other, and more closely than the President's final revision, differs from the Hay manuscript in several instances, but materially only in the words ' under God,' which were interpolated by the President as he spoke, for the phrase does not appear either in the Nicolay or the Hay manuscript, and in the use of 'the' instead of 'this' before 'government of the people.'"

In explaining how this happened, Lambert claimed, "Nicolay says that a few days after the visit to Gettysburg, upon receipt from Mr. Wills of a request on behalf of the States interested in the National Cemetery for the original manuscript of the Dedication Address, the President reexamined his original draft and the version that had appeared in the newspapers, and he saw that because of the variations between them, the first, that is, the Nicolay, seemed incomplete and the others imperfect; he therefore directed his secretaries to make copies of the several reports of the Associated Press and, ' comparing these with his original draft and with his own fresh recollection of the form in which he delivered it, he made a new autograph copy, a careful and deliberate revision.' What became of this first revision is unknown, it was not received by Mr. Wills, who wrote me years ago: 'I did not make a copy of my report of President Lincoln's speech at Gettysburg from a transcript from the original, but from one of the press reports. I have since always used the revised copy furnished the Baltimore fair, of which I have a facsimile in lithograph.'"

The final version mentioned is likely the Hay Copy. According to Lambert, "Another manuscript exists, which is now in the possession of the family of the late John Hay, who as one of the President's private secretaries was present at the dedication. This manuscript, which is in the President's autograph, is reproduced in facsimile in Putnam's Magazine for February, 1909, in connection with 'Recollections of Lincoln' by Gen. James Grant Wilson, who believes the manuscript was written after the President's return from Gettysburg. The Hay manuscript is undoubtedly the second existing draft of the address, but because of information obtained from Col. John P. Nicholson, to whom it was imparted by Secretary Hay, I am convinced that this manuscript was written before November 19, 1863, and that it was inadvertently left at Washington. This opinion is further strengthened by the internal evidence of the manuscript itself."

A picture of the Hay copy with Lincoln's revisions marked in it

Note that the first and third copies mentioned here were in Lincoln's own hand. A third copy, also written by Lincoln, was sent to Everett at the latter's request. Nicolay added, "The last of these, is the regular outgrowth of the two which preceded it and is the perfected product of the President's rhetorical and literary mastery."

Of course, the biggest problem stemming from the existence of the different copies is that they are far from identical, even among those written by Lincoln himself. Lambert explained, "The variations between the several contemporary versions of the Address and its many subsequent reproductions are remarkable, particularly in view of its brevity and importance. Attention has more than once been attracted to these variations; and because of the differences between the earlier reports and the version published in autographic facsimile in 1864, it has been assumed that the discrepancies were due either to blunders on the part of reporters, or to their attempts to improve the President's composition. But examination of a number of versions forces the conclusion that while some of the minor variations in the newspaper reports were caused by typographical or telegraphic errors, the rhetorical differences between these reports and the later version were plainly the result of the author's own revision. The reports of the Address, published November 20, 1863, in the Ledger, the North American, the Press, and the Bulletin of this city, in the Tribune and the Herald of New York, in the Advertiser and the Journal of Boston, and in the Springfield Republican, and on the 23d in the Cincinnati Commercial, were furnished by the Associated Press. The reports printed in the Philadelphia papers named agree with the exception of obvious misprints. The New York papers agree with a single exception, probably a typographical error; the Boston papers also agree substantially with but three verbal variations. But the respective versions of the several cities differ from each other in a number of details, probably because of errors in telegraphing the reports from Gettysburg."

For a while, it didn't really matter which version of the Gettysburg Address was seen as the most accurate, but by the turn of the 20th century, there had developed a move across the country to have the Gettysburg Address inscribed on various plaques on buildings and in military cemeteries. At this point, the Quartermaster General of the United States was tasked with deciding which version should be used, and he narrowed his choices down in 1909:

> "1. The final revision published in *Autograph Leaves of Our Country's Authors*,' prepared by President Lincoln five months after the address for the soldiers' and sailors' fair at Baltimore. This is a version desired by both Col. Nicholson and Robert T. Lincoln. The latter regarded it as representing his father's last and best thoughts as to the address. [Lincoln handwrote two more copies of the Address to be used for this project. They are known as the Bancroft Copy and the Bliss Copy]

> 2. The version stipulated to be used by the act of Feb. 11, 1895, appropriating $5,000 for the bronze tablet containing the address to be erected in the Gettysburg National Park. This differs slightly from the Baltimore Version.

> 3. The John Hay version, from a photographic facsimile of the original manuscript as written and corrected by President Lincoln four days after he had delivered the address and presented it to John Hay. This differs in several particulars from either of the above versions."

The Quartermaster General ultimately decided to pass the buck: "In view of the discrepancies which appear in the several versions of this address, the matter is resubmitted with the request for a decision as to the one which shall be used for the tablets in the national cemeteries."

Then there was the matter of the differences in the versions published in newspapers across the country. As Lambert pointed out, "The reports of the Address published in the Philadelphia Inquirer and in the Cincinnati Gazette, November 20 and 21 respectively, differ materially from each other and from the Associated Press report, and are apparently independent in source ; lacking in completeness, they seem to be paraphrases rather than literal reports, and are probably free renderings of notes made at the time, but are valuable so far as they go, in aiding to determine which of the other reports most nearly represents the words actually spoken. Another independent report of greater value is that made by the Massachusetts Commissioners, which they assert is " in the correct form as the words actually spoken by the President, with great deliberation, were taken down by one of" themselves. The differences between their report and that printed in the North American, which is freer from obvious errors than any other version of the Associated Press report that I have seen, are slight."

Without the debate being definitively settled, the controversy continued. Colonel J. P. Nicholson, then chairman of the Gettysburg National Park Commission, complained to the Quartermaster General: "We are not aware of the source from which the address was obtained in the act creating the National Park, but, word for word, it follows the Baltimore version. The punctuation, however, is the work of the public printer, and is in accordance with the rules of punctuation followed in his office. Colonel Lincoln [Abraham Lincoln's only surviving son, Robert] is undoubtedly correct in his contention of the manner in which the address should be printed, and the Baltimore version as given in the 'Autograph Leaves' should be used and none other. As no tablet has been cast for the Gettysburg National Park there is none to change. When it is cast for the park it will follow, with the approval of the Secretary of War, the Baltimore version."

Robert Lincoln, Lincoln's eldest son and the only one to reach adulthood, also weighed in. He wrote to the Quartermaster General, "As I wrote you before, the Baltimore fair version represents my father's last and best thought as to the address, and the corrections in it were legitimate for an author, and I think there is no doubt they improve the version as written out for Col. Hay. And, as I said to you before, I earnestly hope that the Baltimore fair version will be used. It differs, as you indicate, very slightly from your exhibit A. which, as you say, is given in the statutes-at-large, making an appropriation for the tablet at the Gettysburg National Cemetery. But the statute version was not made, of course, by any responsible person, and I think its incorrections should not be perpetuated when we have, as I have indicated, an exact thing to go by. I am quite sure as a lawyer that there is no obligation upon you, in the new tablets you are making to follow the errors in the text in this old statute, and I trust that you will not do so. I have before me as I write, the book published by the Baltimore Sanitary Fair, which contains a full-sized lithographic reproduction of the address as my father sent to the fair to be used for its benefit."

Finally, the Secretary of War decided that the Baltimore Fair Version of the Gettysburg Address would become and remain the official version "for use on all the tablets to be erected in the national cemeteries as well as for the proposed memorial at Gettysburg. It is proposed to place the latter tablet as near as possible to the exact spot where the martyred President stood when he delivered the address."

Nevertheless, the importance of the Gettysburg Address and the brevity has ensured that people are still obsessed with determining the words exactly as Lincoln delivered them. As Lambert pointed out, "In an address so brief, but so momentous, every syllable tells; and though the differences between the final revision and the speech as actually delivered are few and seemingly immaterial, the changes intensify its strength and pathos and add to its beauty, and as so revised the speech cannot be too jealously preserved as the ultimate expression of the author's sublime thought. Increasing appreciation of Lincoln's character and of his fitness for the great work to which in the providence of God he was called enhances the value of his every word, and surely the form by which he intended this utterance should be judged is that in which we should perpetuate the Gettysburg Address."

Online Resources

The Greatest Battles in History: The Battle of Gettysburg by Charles River Editors

Bibliography

Barton, William E. (1950). *Lincoln at Gettysburg: What He Intended to Say; What He Said; What he was Reported to have Said; What he Wished he had Said.* New York: Peter Smith.

Boritt, Gabor (2006). *The Gettysburg Gospel: The Lincoln Speech That Nobody Knows* Simon & Schuster.

Gramm, Kent. (2001) *November: Lincoln's Elegy at Gettysburg.* Bloomington: Indiana University Press.

Kunhardt, Philip B., Jr. (1983) *A New Birth of Freedom: Lincoln at Gettysburg.* Little Brown & Co.

Reid, Ronald F. "Newspaper Responses to the Gettysburg Addresses". *Quarterly Journal of Speech* 1967 53(1): 50–60.

White, Ronald C. Jr. (2005) *The Eloquent President: A Portrait of Lincoln Through His Words.* New York: Random House. Wills, Garry. (1992) *Lincoln at Gettysburg: The Words That Remade America.* New York: Simon and Schuster.

The Second Inaugural Address

Chapter 1: 1864

Failing to secure the capture of any major northern cities, or the recognition of Great Britain or France, or the complete destruction of any northern armies, the Confederacy's last chance to survive the Civil War was the election of 1864. Democrats had been pushing an anti-war stance or at least a stance calling for a negotiated peace for years, so the South hoped that if a Democrat defeated President Lincoln, or if anti-war Democrats could retake the Congress, the North might negotiate peace with the South. In the election of 1862, anti-war Democrats made some gains in Congress and won the governorship of the State of New York. Confederates were therefore hopeful that trend would continue to the election of 1864.

Although the Army of the Potomac had been victorious at Gettysburg, Lincoln was still upset at what he perceived to be General George Meade's failure to trap Robert E. Lee's Army of Northern Virginia in Pennsylvania. When Lee retreated from Pennsylvania without much fight from the Army of the Potomac, Lincoln was again discouraged, believing Meade had a chance to end the war if he had been bolder. Though historians dispute that, and the Confederates actually invited attack during their retreat, Lincoln was constantly looking for more aggressive fighters to lead his men.

Lincoln's appreciation for aggressive fighters had made him a defender of Ulysses S. Grant as far back as 1862. In April 1862, Grant's army had won the biggest battle in the history of North America to date at Shiloh, with nearly 24,000 combined casualties among the Union and Confederate forces. Usually the winner of a major battle is hailed as a hero, but Grant was hardly a winner at Shiloh. The Battle of Shiloh took place before costlier battles at places like Antietam and Gettysburg, so the extent of the casualties at Shiloh shocked the nation. Moreover, at Shiloh the casualties were viewed as needless; Grant was pilloried for allowing the Confederates to take his forces by surprise, as well as the failure to build defensive earthworks and fortifications, which nearly resulted in a rout of his army. Speculation again arose that Grant had a drinking problem, and some even assumed he was drunk during the battle. Though the Union won, it was largely viewed that their success owed to the heroics of General William Tecumseh Sherman in rallying the men and Don Carlos Buell arriving with his army, and General Buell was happy to receive the credit at Grant's expense.

As a result of the Battle of Shiloh, General Halleck demoted Grant to second-in-command of all armies in his department, an utterly powerless position. And when word of what many considered a "colossal blunder" reached Washington, several congressmen insisted that Lincoln replace Grant in the field. Lincoln famously defended Grant, telling critics, "I can't spare this man. He fights."

Lincoln may have defended Grant, but he found precious few supporters, and the negative attention bothered Grant so much that it is widely believed he turned to alcohol again. While historians still debate that, what is known is that he considered resigning his commission, only to be dissuaded from doing so by General Sherman. While Grant was at the low point of his career, Sherman's career had been resurrected, and he was promoted to major-general the following month. With rumors that Grant was falling off the wagon with alcohol, Sherman tried to reassure Grant not to quit the war, telling him "some happy accident might restore you to favor and your true place." Sherman's appreciation of Grant's faith in his abilities cemented his loyalty and established a friendship between the two that would last a lifetime. In later years Sherman would say, "General Grant is a great general! He stood by me when I was crazy, and I stood by him when he was drunk; and now, sir, we stand by each other always."

Although Grant stayed in the army, it's unclear what position he would have held if Lincoln had not called Halleck to Washington to serve as general-in-chief in July 1862. At the same time, Halleck was given that position in large measure due to Grant's successes in the department under Halleck's command. Thankfully for the Union, Halleck's departure meant that Grant was reinstated as commander.

Lincoln's steadfastness ensured that Grant's victories out West continued to pile up, and after Vicksburg and Chattanooga, Grant had effectively ensured Union control of the states of Kentucky and Tennessee, as well as the entire Mississippi River. Thus, at the beginning of 1864, Lincoln put him in charge of all federal armies, a position that required Grant to come east.

Grant had already succeeded in achieving two of President Lincoln's three primary directives for a Union victory: the opening of the Mississippi Valley Basin, and the domination of the corridor from Nashville to Atlanta. If he could now seize Richmond, he would achieve the third.

Before beginning the Overland Campaign against Lee's army, Grant, Sherman and Lincoln devised a new strategy that would eventually implement total war tactics. Grant aimed to use the Army of the Potomac to attack Lee and/or take Richmond. Meanwhile, General Sherman, now in command of the Department of the West, would attempt to take Atlanta and strike through Georgia. In essence, having already cut the Confederacy in half with Vicksburg campaign, he now intended to bisect the eastern half.

On top of all that, Grant and Sherman were now intent on fully depriving the Confederacy of the ability to keep fighting. By 1864, things were looking so bleak for the South that the Confederate war strategy was simply to ensure Lincoln lost reelection that November, with the hope that a new Democratic president would end the war and recognize the South's independence. With that, and given the shortage in manpower, Lee's strategic objective was to continue defending Richmond, while hoping that Grant would commit some blunder that would allow him a chance to seize an opportunity.

In August 1864, Sherman moved his forces west across Atlanta and then south of it, positioning his men to cut off Atlanta's supply lines and railroads. When the Confederate attempts to stop the maneuvering failed, the writing was on the wall. On September 1, 1864,

John Bell Hood and the Army of Tennessee evacuated Atlanta and torched everything of military value. On September 3, 1864, Sherman famously telegrammed Lincoln, "Atlanta is ours and fairly won." Two months later, so was Lincoln's reelection.

Around the same time Lincoln was winning reelection, Sherman's march to the sea, one of the best known campaigns of the Civil War, was taking place. When he successfully took Savannah, he telegraphed Lincoln to offer the city as a "Christmas gift." Lincoln responded, "Many, many thanks for your Christmas gift – the capture of Savannah. When you were leaving Atlanta for the Atlantic coast, I was anxious, if not fearful; but feeling that you were the better judge, and remembering that 'nothing risked, nothing gained' I did not interfere. Now, the undertaking being a success, the honour is all yours; for I believe none of us went farther than to acquiesce. And taking the work of Gen. Thomas into the count, as it should be taken, it is indeed a great success." Lincoln's reference to "the work of Gen. Thomas" was alluding to arguably the most decisive battle of the entire Civil War. Sherman's Atlanta Campaign and March to the Sea will forever overshadow what George H. Thomas accomplished at the end of 1864, but the Franklin-Nashville campaign may have been the most lopsided of the war, and it all but destroyed the last major Confederate Army west of the Appalachians.

By the beginning of 1865, the Confederacy was in utter disarray. The main Confederate army in the West under John Bell Hood had been nearly destroyed by General Thomas' men at the Battle of Franklin in late 1864, and Sherman's army faced little resistance as it marched through the Carolinas. Although Confederate leaders remained optimistic, by the summer of 1864 they had begun to consider desperate measures in an effort to turn around the war. From 1863-1865, Confederate leaders had even debated whether to conscript black slaves and enlist them as soldiers. Even as their fortunes looked bleak, the Confederates refused to issue an official policy to enlist blacks, and it was likely too late to save the Confederacy anyway.

Thus, by the time Lincoln delivered his Second Inaugural Address in March 1865, the end of the war was in sight. That month, Lincoln would famously met with Grant, Sherman, and Admiral David Porter at City Point, Grant's headquarters during the siege, to discuss how to handle the end of the war.

George Healy's famous painting of the meeting

150 years after the fact, it can be difficult to remember that Lincoln was hardly popular in America in 1865. Indeed, readers who have been steeped in the almost deified legend of Abraham Lincoln often have a hard time comprehending the circumstances under which he was elected for his second term of office. At the time, just weeks before his assassination and promotion to patriotic martyr, the Great Emancipator was quite unpopular. In fact, one article that ran the day of his inauguration criticized the president: "Notwithstanding the recent successes of our armies and the brilliant operations of that dashing leader, Sherman,—and notwithstanding the confidence implied in the re-election of Mr. Lincoln, it is true, nevertheless, that neither himself, his administration nor his policy, command the love, confidence or respect of the great body of the people—no, not even of those who voted for him, It is universally conceded now that his financial policy, on which he must rely for the sinews of war, has been mischievous and & failure,— that his negro policy is about to become a source of still greater mischiefs and a failure even more complete,—and his prosecution of a 'vigorous war,' has ever broken to the hopes of the people the grand promises which it whispered in their ears, and there is too much reason to fear that oven now in North Carolina is impending the greatest calamity and failure of the whole war."

Lincoln's reputation overseas was no better. Great Britain was still furious over the blockade of the Confederate ports and had little affection for the American president. The *Evening Herald* in London complained on March 4, "ABRAHAM LINCOLN is this day proclaimed, for the second time, President of the United States. The honor denied to JOHN ADAMS the elder, and to his son, the ablest and most honorable members of the party from which the Republicans have derived their least disgraceful traditions and their least unworthy principles, is bestowed on one whose insignificance alone was the cause of his original elevation. The honor refused to every one of the successors of General JACKSON is accorded to the meanest and weakest among them. The merit of breaking up the Union and forcing on a wicked, cruel, murderous civil war, is rewarded by the greatest boon which the Republic can bestow."

Chapter 2: The Backdrop of Concerns

"ONLY against the backdrop of...concerns can we appreciate the daring, almost the effrontery, of the Second Inaugural's most obvious characteristic — its extreme brevity. It is true that the Gettysburg Address is even briefer...but that was given at a ceremonial occasion for which Lincoln was not even the principal speaker. No one expected serious discussion of national imperatives when the business of the day was honoring fallen soldiers. It is a different matter when a presidential address is given during a war that is collapsing into a potentially more divisive peace. Yet Lincoln almost breezily dismissed questions of both war and peace, saying that nothing in either called for lengthy treatment. Was he not able to appreciate the scale of the difficulties facing him? Did he think he could reduce them to manageable size by ignoring or belittling them? That this bold defiance of expectation was deliberate is clear from the pride Lincoln took in this speech. ... He clearly knew that he had done well; but he expected to do even better in the years ahead — years he would not be given. He believed he had already equaled or surpassed the Gettysburg Address at least once — in his Second Inaugural." - Historian Garry Wills

Though he had to have been relieved by his reelection, Lincoln did not seem overly enthused about another term when he wrote to the Notification Committee upon receiving the official word of his reelection: "Having served four years in the depths of a great, and yet unended national peril, I can view this call to a second term, in nowise more flatteringly to myself, than as an expression of the public judgment, that I may better finish a difficult work, in which I have labored from the first, than could any one less severely schooled to the task. In this view, and with assured reliance on that Almighty Ruler who has so graciously sustained us thus far; and with increased gratitude to the generous people for their continued confidence, I accept the renewed trust, with its yet onerous and perplexing duties and responsibilities. Please communicate this to the two Houses of Congress."

Assuming he would be running the country for another four years, during which the war would end and he would have the outrageous burden of trying to reunite the Union, Lincoln had plenty of political issues on his mind as he prepared for his second inauguration. However, there were also plenty of personal issues; by March 1865, Lincoln had been exhausted by his work, and he had lost a son during his first term in the White House. In conjunction with that, his wife's grief over that loss continued to burden him. His health was not good, and some doctors have since speculated that Lincoln may have died in office even if he had not been assassinated.

Lincoln was plagued by doubts about how to govern the country, and he often didn't see eye to eye with members of his own Republican Party, but he retained a strong sense of duty, and of course, he was a great orator who knew the power of the spoken word. As Ronald White pointed out in *Lincoln's Greatest Speech: The Second Inaugural*, "Lincoln grew to maturity in a culture that put a priority on the spoken word. He learned how to be heard in that culture. Whether he was addressing the Young Men's Lyceum of Springfield in 1838, or debating Stephen Douglas in 1858, both friend and foe came to respect his rhetorical skills. Whether speaking on behalf of himself or others, Lincoln learned early how to persuade an audience that would vote with their feet if they did not like the speaker's manner or content."

In addition to the influence his upbringing, Lincoln had seen firsthand the impact of his two minute speech at Gettysburg a little over a year earlier. Though he initially thought that speech fell flat, it became popular enough over the next year that he was asked several times to write out a personal copy for others.

In many ways, Lincoln found himself in a unique situation as 1864 gave way to 1865. For one thing, he was only the 6th of 16 presidents to earn a second term in office, and it had been more than 30 years since that last president had been reelected. The last president to do so, Andrew Jackson, had said in his second inaugural address:

> "Fellow-Citizens:
> THE will of the American people, expressed through their unsolicited suffrages, calls me before you to pass through the solemnities preparatory to taking upon myself the duties of President of the United States for another term. For their approbation of my public conduct through a period which has not been without its difficulties, and for this renewed expression of their confidence in my good intentions, I am at a loss for terms adequate to the expression of my gratitude. It shall be displayed to the extent of my humble abilities in continued efforts so to administer the Government as to preserve their liberty and promote their happiness."

Before the brash and aggressive Jackson, there had been the studious, aristocratic James Monroe, who came into office not long after the end of the War of 1812. He had used his second inaugural address to review how he had dealt with America's former enemies: "As soon as the war had terminated, the nation, admonished by its events, resolved to place itself in a situation which should be better calculated to prevent the recurrence of a like evil, and, in case it should recur, to mitigate its calamities. With this view, after reducing our land force to the basis of a peace establishment, which has been further modified since, provision was made for the construction of fortifications at proper points through the whole extent of our coast and such an augmentation of our naval force as should be well adapted to both purposes. The laws making this provision were passed in 1815 and 1816, and it has been since the constant effort of the Executive to carry them into effect."

Then there was James Madison who, like Lincoln, was reelected during an unpopular war being waged on American soil. He used his address to both defend the War of 1812 and castigate America's enemies, the British: "As the war was just in its origin and necessary and noble in its objects, we can reflect with a proud satisfaction that in carrying it on no principle of justice or honor, no usage of civilized nations, no precept of courtesy or humanity, have been infringed. The war has been waged on our part with scrupulous regard to all these obligations, and in a spirit of liberality which was never surpassed. How little has been the effect of this example on the conduct of the enemy!"

Before Madison, Jefferson had spoken of the influence of faith in the nation, and on his dealings with the Native Americans:

"In matters of religion I have considered that its free exercise is placed by the Constitution independent of the powers of the General Government. I have therefore undertaken on no occasion to prescribe the religious exercises suited to it, but have left them, as the Constitution found them, under the direction and discipline of the church or state authorities acknowledged by the several religious societies.

"The aboriginal inhabitants of these countries I have regarded with the commiseration their history inspires. Endowed with the faculties and the rights of men, breathing an ardent love of liberty and independence, and occupying a country which left them no desire but to be undisturbed, the stream of overflowing population from other regions directed itself on these shores; without power to divert or habits to contend against it, they have been overwhelmed by the current or driven before it; now reduced within limits too narrow for the hunter's state, humanity enjoins us to teach them agriculture and the domestic arts; to encourage them to that industry which alone can enable them to maintain their place in existence and to prepare them in time for that state of society which to bodily comforts adds the improvement of the mind and morals. We have therefore liberally furnished them with the implements of husbandry and household use; we have placed among them instructors in the arts of first necessity, and they are covered with the aegis of the law against aggressors from among ourselves."

The first president to be reelected, of course, was George Washington, who had set the precedent for delivering an inaugural address in the first place. On the occasion of his reelection,

Washington spoke fewer than 150 words.

In preparing his own second inaugural address, Lincoln would find inspiration in all these men, and in others. Lincoln was clearly influenced by Washington's brevity, as his speech, unlike many others made by leaders in his situation, was only 700 words long. Nonetheless, he was determined to pack as much punch into those 700 words as he could. Therefore, he carefully considered a number of sources of inspiration, including those of Andrew Jackson, whose modest yet forthright acceptance of his reelection likely shaped Lincoln's first paragraph: "At this second appearing to take the oath of the Presidential office there is less occasion for an extended address than there was at the first. Then a statement somewhat in detail of a course to be pursued seemed fitting and proper." In fact, Lincoln seems to have paid minimum attention to his opening remarks, as if he was anxious to move on to the meet of his speech.

One thing that anyone studying Lincoln's second inaugural address should remember is that while he was self-educated, Lincoln still had the advantages that go along with a classical education, including a deep understanding of history and access to many of the great works of classical literature. He was something of an amateur admirer of William Shakespeare, and much of what he wrote, especially in the second inaugural address, was influenced by Shakespearean thought and language. Both Lincoln and Shakespeare were influenced by the language and imagery of the Bible, and in speaking of his own interest in Shakespeare, Lincoln himself once admitted, "Some of Shakespeare's plays I have never read; while others I have gone over perhaps as frequently as any unprofessional reader. Among the latter are Lear, Richard Third, Henry Eighth, Hamlet, and especially Macbeth. I think nothing equals Macbeth. It is wonderful.... I think the soliloquy in Hamlet commencing 'O, my offense is rank' surpasses that commencing 'To be, or not to be.'" Likewise, James Randell, who wrote a popular biography of Lincoln, maintained that the president "not only used a great many Shakespearean allusions, but he also discussed problems of interpretation, with remarkable insight, and gave effective performances of his own."

Chapter 3: Religious Beliefs

"The subject of Abraham Lincoln's religious beliefs has occupied students of Lincoln lore since 1865. Some historians, for example, have noted that Lincoln's religious outlook was influenced by the American puritan religious tradition. Other writers have maintained that, after his New Salem sojourn (1831-1837), Lincoln underwent a conversion experience and became a Christian. Partly in response to this type of contention, Lincoln's law partner, William H. Herndon, was at pains to contend that Lincoln had died as he had lived, "an unbeliever" (Current, 55). But virtually no published writer has suggested that Lincoln's religious views were seriously influenced by the ideas expressed in the works of William Shakespeare. Yet, once Shakespeare's influence on Lincoln is acknowledged, it provides a new focus for understanding Lincoln's religious outlook and his March 4, 1865, religious utterances in the Second Inaugural Address." - James Stevenson, author of *A Providential Theology: Shakespeare's Influence on Lincoln's*

Second Inaugural Address

One of the things that Lincoln knew from experience was that when he appealed to the American people on a moral, spiritual level, he was usually successful, but for his own part, at least according to historian Glen Thurow, Lincoln's faith was "conditional." Thurow continued, "One can see the kinship of the Second Inaugural to that skepticism for which Lincoln was noted among his friends. The faith that regards providence as essentially unknowable and the skepticism of all providence agree that the pattern of future events cannot be known and hence that our capacity to manage the future is limited." Lincoln himself once wrote, "The will of God prevails. In great contests each party claims to act in accordance with the will of God. Both may be, and one must be wrong. God cannot be for, and against the same thing at the same time. In the present civil war it is quite possible that God's purpose is something different from the purpose of either party— and yet the human instrumentalities, working just as they do, are of the best adaptation to effect His purpose. I am almost ready to say this is probably true— that God wills this contest, and wills that it shall not end yet. By his mere quiet power, on the minds of the now contestants, He could have either saved or destroyed the Union without a human contest. Yet the contest began. And having begun He could give the final victory to either side any day. Yet the contest proceeds."

It is fairly well known that Lincoln was not the most religious of the 19th century presidents, and he often had a fragile sense of faith. That said, he also seemed to take religious cues from Shakespeare, as James Stevenson pointed out: "So, from the 1830s to early 1865, Lincoln made clear that Shakespeare, and not John Calvin, best expressed his understanding of man's subordination to a Providential design. In effect, Lincoln adopted the outlook of the Renaissance neo-Stoics who had reconciled their view of Christianity with their philosophy of fate to arrive at the idea of a Providence which accepted both fate and free will. Just as historian Robert Hoopes noted in regard to the poetry of John Milton, the verses of Shakespeare reflected a synthesis of the 'voices of classical Antiquity, the Middle Ages, and the Renaissance' which rejected 'the extremes' of Catholicism and Calvinism. The resulting Christian humanism appealed to a man of Lincoln's mild yet fatalistic temperament. By the time Lincoln delivered his Second Inaugural Address, the idea of a Providential design dominated his thinking on the Civil War. Already, at Gettysburg, his rhetoric had turned in a profoundly religious direction. Therefore, as the slaughter continued, it impelled greater religious reflection…And when the Second Inaugural Address is considered, it is evident that the Address reflected the deeply spiritual poetic side of Lincoln more than any of his other public statements. Shakespeare's influence is unmistakable, for Lincoln not only crafted his speech with the cadence and rhythm of late sixteenth- and early seventeenth-century English poetry, but, like Shakespeare, he struck a richer poetic meaning with his tone. In gloomy middle passages of oration, one hears the voice of Hamlet or Macbeth just as surely as one hears the preaching of ancient biblical prophets. And, given his agonized imagination and poetic sensitivity, the Second Inaugural Address became the culminating expression of Lincoln's lifetime cathartic experiences."

In fact, Stevenson maintained that "in presenting his entire theological discussion, Lincoln expressed such a pronounced Shakespearean view of history that Richmond's last words in Richard III could well have served as the thematic model for the Second Inaugural's final three paragraphs. Thus, in his attempt to lead his embittered fellow countrymen away from thoughts of vengeance, Lincoln argued that the war had been bloody, but God's justice had been done. Similarly, as if anticipating Lincoln's Address, Richmond was conventionally pious. With Richard III vanquished, Richmond's first words in the play's last scene acknowledged proper homage to God: 'God and your arms be prais'd, victorious friends.' Continuing, Richmond expressed concern for the dead: 'Inter their bodies as become their births;' he offered mercy to his former foes: 'Proclaim a pardon to the soldiers fled / That in submission will return to us;' he thanked God for a return to the proper earthly order. ... And, finally, Richmond resolved to heal the wounds of civil war:' Now civil wounds are stopp'd, peace lives again; / That she may long live here, God say amen.'"

Stevenson viewed Lincoln's speech as designed, at least in part, to let even his most Calvinistic listeners know that the Civil War was not caused by God's will but by man's evil, citing Lincoln's "stunning four-word conclusion": "On the occasion corresponding to this four years ago, all thoughts were anxiously directed to an impending civil-war. All dreaded it--all sought to avert it.... Both parties deprecated war; but one of them would make war rather than let the nation survive; and the other would accept war rather than let it perish. And the war came."

Of course, no matter how much he was influenced by Shakespeare and presidential predecessors, Lincoln's words and ideas were still his own, and in looking through his letters, it's possible to see how his ideas developed. As Garry Wills noted, "THE problem with compromise [concerning Reconstruction] on this scale is that it seems morally neutral, open even to injustices if they work. Answering that objection was the task Lincoln set himself in the Second Inaugural. Everything said there was meant to prove that pragmatism was, in this situation, not only moral but pious. Men could not pretend to have God's adjudicating powers. People had acted for mixed motives on all sides of the civil conflict just past. The perfectly calibrated punishment or reward for each leader, each soldier, each state, could not be incorporated into a single political disposition of the problems. ... Abstract principle can lead to the attitude Fiat iustitia, ruat coelum — 'Justice be done, though it bring down the cosmos.' Lincoln had learned to have a modest view of his ability to know what ultimate justice was, and to hesitate before bringing down the whole nation in its pursuit. He asked others to recognize in the intractability of events the disposing hand of a God with darker, more compelling purposes than any man or group of men could foresee. This lesson, learned from the war, he meant to apply to the equally intractable problems of the peace."

Wills then went on to observe, "In fact, the whole Second Inaugural was already present, in germ, in his letter of April 4, 1864, to Albert G. Hodges, a newspaper editor in Kentucky." In that letter, Lincoln had written, "I claim not to have controlled events, but confess plainly that events have controlled me. Now, at the end of three years struggle the nation's condition is not what either party, or any man devised, or expected. God alone can claim it. Whither it is tending seems plain. If God now wills the removal of a great wrong, and wills also that we of the North as well as you of the South, shall pay fairly for our complicity in that wrong, impartial history will find therein new cause to attest and revere the justice and goodness of God."

These were reflections very important to him. At the Sanitary Fair (an early form of Red Cross activity) in Baltimore on April 18, 1864, Lincoln said, "When the war began, three years ago, neither party, nor any man, expected it would last till now. Each looked for the end, in some way, long ere to—day. Neither did any anticipate that domestic slavery would be much affected by the war. But here we are; the war has not ended, and slavery has been much affected—how much needs not now to be recounted. So true is it that man proposes, and God disposes. But we can see the past, though we may not claim to have directed it; and seeing it, in this case, we feel more hopeful and confident for the future. The world has never had a good definition of the word liberty, and the American people, just now, are much in want of one. We all declare for liberty; but in using the same word we do not all mean the same thing. With some the word liberty may mean for each man to do as he pleases with himself, and the product of his labor; while with others the same word may mean for some men to do as they please with other men, and the product of other men's labor. Here are two, not only different, but incompatible things, called by the same name—liberty. And it follows that each of the things is, by the respective parties, called by two different and incompatible names—liberty and tyranny."

Also in September 1864, Lincoln explained some of his ideas about the role of God in the lives of men when he wrote to Eliza Gurney, a Quaker woman who had earlier visited him: "In all, it has been your purpose to strengthen my reliance on God. I am much indebted to the good Christian people of the country for their constant prayers and consolations; and to no one of them, more than to yourself. The purposes of the Almighty are perfect, and must prevail, though we erring mortals may fail to accurately perceive them in advance. We hoped for a happy termination of this terrible war long before this; but God knows best, and has ruled otherwise. We shall yet acknowledge His wisdom and our own error therein. Meanwhile we must work earnestly in the best light He gives us, trusting that so working still conduces to the great ends He ordains. Surely He intends some great good to follow this mighty convulsion, which no mortal could make, and no mortal could stay."

Chapter 4: Providential Design

"Accordingly, the Second Inaugural Address revealed a theology which perceived the entire nation as a nation of quasi free-will sinners whose crime was so foul that it upset the Providential design. In order to restore that design, God momentarily dominated more of man's limited free will and turned the years of Civil War into a bloody remission for the sin of slavery. But the fact that everyone paid the gruesome price meant that everyone had atoned and that everyone was entitled to forgiveness. Besides, since Lincoln eschewed religious sectarianism, his theology favored an ecumenical outlook. He, like Hamlet, believed that 'There are more things in heaven and earth, ... / Than are dreamt of in your philosophy.' That is why, as Wolf's research found, the words 'Jesus' and 'Savior' do not appear in Lincoln's writings (179-80). Still, while the theology of the Second Inaugural Address is broader than any Christian creed, it is immersed in Judeo-Christian ethics. Thus, when willful men grossly ignore the ethical standards of Divine Providence, they suffer, as surely as do similar characters in Shakespeare's plays, 'the rod of heaven, / To punish [their] mistreadings.' Such is Lincoln's theological concept of 'a divinity that shapes our ends, /Rough-hew them how we will.'" - *James Stevenson*

There was also an obvious sense of his own belief in divine retribution and the hand he was called to play in it. In July 1863, he had issued the Order of Retaliation: "It is the duty of every government to give protection to its citizens, of whatever class, color, or condition, and especially to those who are duly organized as soldiers in the public service. The law of nations and the usages and customs of war as carried on by civilized powers, permit no distinction as to color in the treatment of prisoners of war as public enemies. To sell or enslave any captured person, on account of his color, and for no offence against the laws of war, is a relapse into barbarism and a crime against the civilization of the age. The government of the United States will give the same protection to all its soldiers, and if the enemy shall sell or enslave anyone because of his color, the offense shall be punished by retaliation upon the enemy's prisoners in our possession. It is therefore ordered that for every soldier of the United States killed in violation of the laws of war, a rebel soldier shall be executed; and for every one enslaved by the enemy or sold into slavery, a rebel soldier shall be placed at hard labor on the public works and continued at such labor until the other shall be released and receive the treatment due to a prisoner of war."

According to Stevenson, "Getting even more specific in his next paragraph, Lincoln reinforced his motif that man's free will brought on the war by noting that Southern slave owners had such a 'powerful interest' in maintaining their slave system that they had started the war.' He then went on to quote: 'All knew that this interest was, somehow, the cause of the war. To strengthen, perpetuate, and extend this interest was the object for which the insurgents would rend the Union, even by war; while the government claimed no right to do more than to restrict the territorial enlargement of it.' In Lincoln's mind, it would seem, the entire unfortunate affair was a product of man's greed."

Lincoln did not stop there. Instead, as Stevenson noted, "Lincoln, however, was dissatisfied with a purely secular and material explanation of the war and its causes. So, his next lines remind us that men, as Shakespeare's villain heroes were grieved to learn, do not have complete free will. This means that, from the theological perspective, Lincoln was suggesting that the human actors in the war's unfolding tragedy had lost control of events."

To support this claim, Stevenson needed only to cite Lincoln's comment that "[n]either party expected for the war, the magnitude, or the duration, which it has already attained. Neither anticipated that the cause of the conflict might cease with, or even before, the conflict itself should cease. Each looked for an easier triumph, and a result less fundamental and astounding."

According to Stevenson, one of the things Lincoln was wrestling with was the extent to which man's prayers to God affected the outcome of events. Steeped in traditional American Christianity, he had no doubt been taught to pray as a child. At the same time, he had seen his prayers often go unanswered, especially with the death of his mother Nancy. Certainly, he knew that there were devout Christians on both sides who were each praying for triumph for their own armies. Lincoln mentioned this contradiction in the speech: "Both read the same Bible, and pray to the same God; and each invokes His aid against the other. It may seem strange that any men should dare to ask a just God's assistance in wringing their bread from the sweat of other men's faces; but let us judge not that we be not judged. The prayers of both could not be answered; that of neither has been answered fully. The Almighty has His own purposes." To this end, Stevenson asserted, "With such words, Lincoln was not only contending that God's purposes were different from men's purposes but that God imposed His purposes on men."

In the third paragraph, Lincoln went past Shakespeare and all the way back to the Bible, quoting Matthew 18:7: "Woe unto the world because of offenses! for it must needs be that offenses come; but woe to that man by whom the offense cometh!" In this interpretation, the offense was slavery, and the judgment was being meted out by the Union Army. While Georgia howled over its treatment at the hands of Sherman, and the Union's top generals were implementing total war, this was an important point to make. This same theme could be found in the Union's most famous marching song, "The Battle Hymn of the Republic." As Stevenson put it, "when Lincoln turned God into an angry anti-slavery advocate, he finally aligned himself with individuals like John Brown. Indeed, Lincoln did nothing to soften the retribution tone of the Second Inaugural until the final paragraph of his oration. Hence, when Lincoln expressed the idea that God willed 'this terrible war' to punish both North and South, he was asserting the abolitionist belief that any compromise with slavery was sin itself. ... It also incorporated...Shakespeare's great theme of national prosperity distorted by a crime and civil war."

Following in the path of Shakespearean classics such as King Lear, Hamlet, and Macbeth, Lincoln said in his address, "If we shall suppose that American Slavery is one of those offenses which, in the providence of God, must needs come, but which, having continued through His appointed time, He now wills to remove, and that He gives to both North and South, this terrible war, as the woe due to those by whom the offense came, shall we discern therein any departure from those divine attributes which the believers in a Living God always ascribe to Him?"

Lincoln drew his third and most powerful paragraph to a close by warning the country that God's will, as he interpreted it, would not be outdone, and that the war must continue until it was decisively finished. "Fondly do we hope--fervently do we pray--that this mighty scourge of war may speedily pass away. Yet, if God wills that it continue, until all the wealth piled by the bond-man's two hundred and fifty years of unrequited toil shall be sunk, and until every drop of blood drawn with the lash, shall be paid by another drawn with the sword, as was said three thousand years ago, so still it must be said `the judgments of the Lord, are true and righteous altogether [Psalm 19:9].'"

Finally, Lincoln came to his closing paragraph, where he knew he needed to offer listeners some hope for the future. Given the previous words about the terrible toll of the war and God's role, Lincoln's final words strike a much more conciliatory tone. Moreover, with the Union firmly winning the war and the end seemingly in sight, the inaugural address gave him a chance to offer an olive branch to the defeated South. "With malice toward none; With charity for all; With firmness in the right, As God gives us to see the right, Let us strive on to finish the work we are in; To bind up the nation's wounds; To care for him who shall have borne the battle, And for his widow, and his orphan--To do all which may achieve And cherish a just, and a lasting peace, Among ourselves, and with all nations."

Interestingly enough, this was a concern that was often on Lincoln's mind. In fact, just six months earlier, he had written a letter in which he admitted, "We hoped for a happy termination of this terrible war long before this; but God knows best, and has ruled otherwise. We shall yet acknowledge His wisdom and our own error therein. Meanwhile we must work earnestly in the best light He gives us, trusting that so working still conduces to the great ends He ordains. Surely He intends some great good to follow this mighty convulsion, which no mortal could make, and no mortal could stay."

In Stevenson's opinion, "In both form and meaning, then, the ideas in this paragraph grew out of Lincoln's poetic imagination as well as out of the logic of his previous argument. Almost like Malcolm, at the end of Macbeth, Lincoln's language suggested, 'What's more to do, / Which would be planted newly with the time.' And yet, his words soared magnificently beyond Malcolm's remarks because they climaxed the increasingly spiritual progression of Lincoln's whole Address. With just seventy-five words, Lincoln's prose attained the grace of poetry and called for tolerance, forgiveness, charity, brotherhood, peace, and renewal. Such a poetic peroration of such a religious speech perfectly suited the religious outlook of a man whose wife, Mary, stated: 'He was a religious man by nature.... It was a kind of poetry in his nature.'"

Chapter 5: At the Inauguration

"The President very quietly rode down to the Capitol in his own carriage, by himself, on a sharp trot, about noon, either because he wished to be on hand to sign bills, &c., or to get rid of marching in line with the muslin Temple of Liberty, and the pasteboard Monitor. I saw him on his return, at three o'clock, after the performance was over. He was in his plain two-horse barouche, and looked very much worn and tired; the lines, indeed, of vast responsibilities, intricate questions, and demands of life and death, cut deeper than ever upon his dark brown face; yet all the old goodness, tenderness, sadness, and canny shrewdness, underneath the furrows. ... By his side sat his little boy, of ten years. There were no soldiers, only a lot of civilians on horseback, with huge yellow scarfs over their shoulders, riding around the carriage. At the inauguration four years ago, he rode down and back again surrounded by a dense mass of armed cavalrymen eight deep, with drawn sabers, and carbines clanking at their sides, and there were sharp-shooters stationed at every corner on the route." - Walt Whitman

On the evening of Saturday, March 4, the *Sunday Herald* in Washington issued a Special Dispatch covering the Inauguration. It read, "The inauguration ceremonies of President Lincoln took place today, between the hours of eleven and one o clock, and though not attended by such assemblages or accompanied by such large and brilliant displays as on previous similar occasions, were, nevertheless, rendered prominent and attractive by a large outpouring of people to witness an inaugural procession that, in view of the terrible weather which preceded, was altogether creditable to those composing it. The day opened in Washington with black and lowering clouds and a most violent storm of wind and rain, and occasionally hail, which, during yesterday and last night, had continued without intermission and which rendered the badly paved and unpaved streets almost impassable. By ten o clock, however, the sidewalks were crowded with people who stood in the rain, while every housetop, window, portico, stoop, etc., were occupied by ladies and gentlemen. The long colonnade of the Treasury building bore an immense freight of human beings, and the west front of the Capitol was similarly loaded. Numerous private residences were decorated with the American flag, while the National ensign waved from nearly every housetop from the White House to the Capitol. Cars, omnibuses, carriages, etc., were rendered attractive by a display of miniature flags. The State Department attracted much attention by its brilliant display of gracefully draped flags, as did the War Department by its display of flags and also of arches and other decorations of evergreen."

A picture of Lincoln at the podium

It should surprise no one that the citizens of the weary nation were looking forward to having something to celebrate. As Walt Whitman pointed out in his essay on the day, the changes wrought in the capital on this occasion were both symbolic and eerie. "Simply saying, first, however, that I have this moment been up to look at the gorgeously arrayed ball and supper-rooms, for the Inauguration Dance aforesaid, (which begins in a few hours;) and I could not help thinking of the scene those rooms, where the music will sound and the dancers' feet presently tread—what a different scene they presented to my view a while since, filled with a crowded mass of the worst wounded of the war, brought in from Second Bull Run, Antietam, and Fredericksburg. Tonight, beautiful women, perfumes, the violins' sweetness, the polka and the waltz; but then, the amputation, the blue face, the groan, the glassy eye of the dying, the clotted rag, the odor of the old wounds and blood, and many a mother's son amid strangers, passing away untended there, (for the crowd of the badly hurt was great, and much for nurse to do, and much for surgeon.) Think not of such grim things, gloved ladies, as you bow to your partners, and the figures of the dance this night are loudly called, or you may drop on the floor that has known what this one knew, but two short winters since."

For his part, Whitman found the crowd itself to be more interesting than the dignitaries. Indeed, he seemed aware that there was a symbolism in those present, one that modern readers know would soon be expressed in Lincoln's own words. "As the day advanced, of course Pennsylvania Avenue absorbed all. The show here was to me worth all the rest. The effect was heterogeneous, novel, and quite inspiriting. It will perhaps be got at, by making a list in the following manner, to wit: Mud, (and such mud!) amid and upon which streaming crowds of citizens; lots of blue-dressed soldiers; any quantity of male and female Africans, (especially female;) horrid perpetual entanglements at the crossings, sometimes a dead lock; more mud, the wide street black, and several inches deep with it; clattering groups of cavalrymen out there on a gallop, (and occasionally as single horseman might have been seen, &c;) processions of firemen, with their engines, evidently from the north; a regiment of blacks, in full uniform, with guns on their shoulders; the splendor overhead; the oceanic crowd, equal almost to Broadway; the wide Avenue, its vista very fine, down at one end closed by the capitol, with milky bulging dome, and the Maternal Figure over all, (with the sword by her side and the sun glittering on her helmeted head) at the other, the western end, the pillared front of the Treasury Building, looking south; altogether quite a refreshing spot and hour, and plenty of architectural show with life and magnetism also. Among other items, our heavenly neighbor Hesperus, the star of the West, was quite plain just after midday; it was right over head. I occasionally stopped with the crowds and looked up at it. Every corner had its little squad, thus engaged; often soldiers, often black, with raised faces, well worth looking at themselves, as new styles of physiognomical pictures."

Naturally, the *Dispatch* was less romantic in its description of the event: "The scene along Pennsylvania Avenue about eleven o'clock, as the clouds rolled away and the bright spring sun shone out, was most brilliant indeed. Every vehicle and horse were removed from Pennsylvania Avenue and the broad street unobstructed from curbstone to curbstone. Up to this hour it was deemed doubtful if the ceremonies would take place outdoors, but when the weather gave promise of continued fairness the vast throng pushed on rapidly up Capitol Hill. The sidewalks, grounds, etc., were covered by acres of human beings. The large space in front of the Capitol was stripped of much of the budding material which occupied its broad area, and on the marble blocks plank flooring was laid so that no portion of the grounds was left obstructed. The entrances on the north and south sides of the Park were enlarged, and nothing neglected that was necessary to afford favorable opportunities to the crowd for comfortably witnessing the interesting ceremonies. While every available standing and sitting place at the Capitol end of the avenue was occupied, the crowd gathered in the vicinity of the Presidential mansion was in no wise diminished, for as early as nine o'clock a crowd began to assemble in front of the White House, on Pennsylvania avenue, and in a short time both sides of the street were completely jammed up by those eager to see the President..."

In fact, Lincoln was not at the White House that morning but instead already at the Capitol, where he had to take care of some last minute business with Congress. Thus, the crowd was treated to a procession that included Mrs. Lincoln and other dignitaries. Meanwhile, all was being made ready in the Senate chamber for the swearing in, as no one knew if the weather would let up so that it could take place outside. *The Herald* reported, "The Chamber was arranged at an early hour for the ceremonies. Within the arc formed by the desks around the front of the Vice President's chair, elegant cushioned armed-chairs were placed and cane seats sandwiched between the widely separated chairs of the Senators, while sofas and settees filled up the rear. The proceedings of the Senate were quite uninteresting, and about ten o clock, on motion of Mr. Powell, the doors of the galleries were opened to the ladies. ... The President was seated in front of the Secretary's table and the committee of arrangements were on his left. ... From the Chamber the President and ether dignitaries proceeded to the rotunda and thence to the platform on the Eastern portico, where, before a sea of upturned faces, Mr. Lincoln read his brief inaugural. The scenes of enthusiasm were long and general before and after the reading, though there was profound silence when Chief Justice Chase arose in his judicial robes and administered the oath required by the Constitution."

Finally, Lincoln rose to read the address that he had worked on over the preceding weeks:

> "Fellow Citizens,
>
> AT this second appearing to take the oath of the Presidential office there is less occasion for an extended address than there was at the first. Then a statement somewhat in detail of a course to be pursued seemed fitting and proper. Now, at the expiration of four years, during which public declarations have been constantly called forth on every point and phase of the great contest which still absorbs the attention and engrosses the energies of the nation, little that is new could be presented. The progress of our arms, upon which all else chiefly depends, is as well known to the public as to myself, and it is, I trust, reasonably satisfactory and encouraging to all. With high hope for the future, no prediction in regard to it is ventured.
>
> On the occasion corresponding to this four years ago all thoughts were anxiously directed to an impending civil war. All dreaded it, all sought to avert it. While the inaugural address was being delivered from this place, devoted altogether to saving the Union without war, insurgent agents were in the city seeking to destroy it without war—seeking to dissolve the Union and divide effects by negotiation. Both parties deprecated war, but one of them would make war rather than let the nation survive, and the other would accept war rather than let it perish, and the war came.
>
> One-eighth of the whole population were colored slaves, not distributed

generally over the Union, but localized in the southern part of it. These slaves constituted a peculiar and powerful interest. All knew that this interest was somehow the cause of the war. To strengthen, perpetuate, and extend this interest was the object for which the insurgents would rend the Union even by war, while the Government claimed no right to do more than to restrict the territorial enlargement of it. Neither party expected for the war the magnitude or the duration which it has already attained. Neither anticipated that the cause of the conflict might cease with or even before the conflict itself should cease. Each looked for an easier triumph, and a result less fundamental and astounding. Both read the same Bible and pray to the same God, and each invokes His aid against the other. It may seem strange that any men should dare to ask a just God's assistance in wringing their bread from the sweat of other men's faces, but let us judge not, that we be not judged. The prayers of both could not be answered. That of neither has been answered fully. The Almighty has His own purposes. 'Woe unto the world because of offenses; for it must needs be that offenses come, but woe to that man by whom the offense cometh.' If we shall suppose that American slavery is one of those offenses which, in the providence of God, must needs come, but which, having continued through His appointed time, He now wills to remove, and that He gives to both North and South this terrible war as the woe due to those by whom the offense came, shall we discern therein any departure from those divine attributes which the believers in a living God always ascribe to Him? Fondly do we hope, fervently do we pray, that this mighty scourge of war may speedily pass away. Yet, if God wills that it continue until all the wealth piled by the bondsman's two hundred and fifty years of unrequited toil shall be sunk, and until every drop of blood drawn with the lash shall be paid by another drawn with the sword, as was said three thousand years ago, so still it must be said 'the judgments of the Lord are true and righteous altogether.'

    With malice toward none, with charity for all, with firmness in the right as God gives us to see the right, let us strive on to finish the work we are in, to bind up the nation's wounds, to care for him who shall have borne the battle and for his widow and his orphan, to do all which may achieve and cherish a just and lasting peace among ourselves and with all nations."

Noah Brooks was there that day and witnessed the speech. He later wrote, "Among the memories of a lifetime, doubtless there are none more fondly cherished by those who were so fortunate as to stand near Lincoln at that historic moment than the recollection of the beautiful solemnity, the tender sympathy, of these inspired utterances, and the rapt silence of the thronging multitude. There were many cheers and many tears as this noble address was concluded.

According to Whitman, it seemed in retrospect that even nature itself had conspired to frame

Lincoln's speech in beauty: "On Saturday, a forenoon like whirling demons, dark, with slanting rain, full of rage; and then the afternoon, so calm, so bathed with flooding splendor from heaven's most excellent sun, with atmosphere of sweetness; so clear it showed the stars, long, long before they were due. As the President came out on the capitol portico, a curious little white cloud, the only one in that part of the sky, appeared like a hovering bird, right over him. Indeed, the heavens, the elements, all the meteorological influences, have run riot for weeks past. Such caprices, abruptest alternations of frowns and beauty, I never knew. It is a common remark that (as last Summer was different in its spells of intense heat from any preceding it) the Winter just completed has been without parallel. It has remained so down to the hour I am writing. Much of the daytime of the past month was sulky, with leaden heaviness, fog, interstices of bitter cold, and some insane storms. But there have been samples of another description. Nor earth, nor land ever knew spectacles of superber beauty than some of the nights have lately been here. The Western Star, in the earlier hours of evening, has never been so large, so clear; it seems as if it told something, as if it held rapport indulgent with humanity, with us Americans."

Chapter 6: A Brighter Star in Midday

"When he had finished the speech, to somewhat puzzled cheers and applause, Lincoln took the oath of office. There was a solemnity here that had been lacking in the slobbery performance of Johnson's oath. The day's storm had yielded to dramatic meteorological effects during the speech. A peephole in the dark clouds let some see a bright star in midday. Sun slanted through the lattice of clouds with spotlighting effects. Whitman saw a 'curious little white cloud ... like a hovering bird, right over him.' Despite this breaking of the storm, Lincoln seemed 'very much worn and tired' when Whitman saw his carriage returning, with only Lincoln and his ten-year-old son sitting in it. Later that evening, at the White House reception, Whitman noticed the same sad weariness in the expression of the President (which inhibited Whitman from going up to shake his hand). Lincoln no doubt wondered how many, if any, understood the profound message he had crafted. The response of the crowd was proper, but the religious tone of the speech hardly called for jubilation." - Garry Wills

Following his speech, Lincoln returned as planned to the White House to rest, have something to eat, and prepare for the evening's festivities. Meanwhile, reporters were rushing to telegraph offices around the city to get copies of Lincoln's speech, along with their comments on it, back to their newspaper offices. Two days later, on March 6, *The New York Herald* reported, "At about 1 o'clock, the bands being at last hushed, the President rose and stepped forward to the reading desk. He was greeted with faint applause; indeed, there was no enthusiasm throughout the address. It was not strictly an inaugural address, since it was read before Mr. Lincoln took the oath. It was more like a valedictory. The President read in a very loud, clear voice, and hundreds of the audience could hear it. During the delivery of the speech, Stanton and Seward were remarkably attentive, rising and bending forward to listen. The crowd kept pushing nearer and nearer the platform. Sumner smiled superciliously at the frequent Scriptural quotations. Negroes ejaculated 'bress de Lord, ' in a low murmur, at the end of almost every sentence. Beyond this there was no cheering of any consequence. Even the soldiers did not hurrah much. The statement that 'the progress of our arms is, I trust, reasonably satisfactory and encouraging to all,' met with no response, although the President paused significantly. The declaration that we accepted the war rather than let the nation perish drew the first cheer. The remark that slavery would cease with the war was applauded. The satirical observation that men asked God's assistance in wringing bread from other men's faces caused a half laugh. These were the only marks of approbation until the close of the address. After a brief pause, the President and Chief Justice rose together, and the oath of office was administered. The voice of the Chief Justice was inaudible, but the workings of his countenance could be distinctly seen as he labored to be impressive. Then there was a cheer, and the President came forward and bowed and smiled. During the whole ceremony he looked unusually handsome. When delivering his speech, his face glowed with enthusiasm, and he evidently felt every word that he uttered."

The *Herald* also gave a complimentary description of Lincoln and his presence as a speaker: "Mr. Lincoln is said to be an awkward man. It is to a man's credit to be awkward in some situations, and those are doubtless the situations in which he has been most seen by those who have insisted upon this point in their pictures. He was not at all awkward on the platform in the morning, where in front of an assemblage, representative in some degree of the people of every state, he gave utterance to the few eloquent sentences that make up his address. The tall form was in harmony with the scene, and its bold outline served only to distinguish him as the man above all others of that grand occasion. Here (inaugural reception) he is awkward; but the awkwardness is due to the situation, which is a mean and unnatural one. He would be a mean and small man who would not be more or less awkward in it. Shakespeare has presented us with this very situation, and has shown us how it affects a large-headed man; for Coriolanus before the Roman people is not so much a politician as a man of simple nature, who revolts at the artificial idea that he must be shaken by the hand by Tom, Dick and Harry, simply because he is of all the Romans the man most fit to be consul. It is certain that Mr. Lincoln discharged this duty with a divine patience."

Meanwhile, the Washington paper *National Intelligencer* raved on March 6: "We desire no better words from the President for our platform than compose the concluding paragraph of his Inaugural Address. They are equally distinguished for patriotism, statesmanship, and benevolence, and deserve to be printed in gold." The *New York Times* article, printed the same day, agreed: "The President, in assuming the responsibilities of his second term, indulges in but few words. He makes no boasts of what he has done, or promises of what he will do. He does not re-expound the principles of the war; does not re-declare the worth of the Union; does not re-proclaim that absolute submission to the Constitution is the only peace. All that he does is simply to advert to the cause of the war, and ... to recognize in solemn language the righteous judgment of Heaven; and to drop an earnest exhortation that all will now stand by the right, and strive for a peace that shall be just and lasting."

The Boston Evening Transcript also praised Lincoln: "The President's Inaugural is a singular state paper — made so by the times. No similar document has ever been published to the world. . . . The President was lifted above the level upon which political rules usually stand, and felt himself 'in the very presence of the very mystery of Providence.'"

The *Wilmington Delaware State Journal & Statesman* said of Lincoln's Address, "It is the most concise document of the kind that ever emanated from the Chief Magistrate of the Nation. It is, however, full of wisdom and breathes a pure spirit of patriotism and lofty sentiment which will call forth the admiration of all who read it." The *Philadelphia Inquirer* was even more direct: "The address is characteristic of Mr. Lincoln. It exhibits afresh the kindness of his heart, and the large charity which has ever marked his actions toward those who are his personal enemies as well as the enemies of his country. Yet he is firm and will not deviate from the straight line of duty. The American people will appreciate the plain manly speech of the President, and will join with him in his efforts 'to finish the work we are in....'"

On March 7, the *Sacramento Daily Union* opined, "To President Lincoln, if we may judge by the telegraphic report of his second inaugural address, the hour of apparent victory is the hour for a more solemn acknowledgement of our indebtedness to Divine Providence, a clearer recognition of the cause of the national affliction, and a sterner resolution to merit the blessing of peace and prosperity hereafter by purging the land of a national sin. . . . The reverential tone and intense appreciation of the truth blazoned by the war that impartial liberty is the life of the republic and the guarantee of peace, are the noteworthy features of this address to the American people."

Similarly, the *Jersey City Times* proclaimed, "President Lincoln's Inaugural address has, doubtless, ere this been read by nearly all our readers — but too many copies of it cannot be printed or circulated, and it ought to be in all American homes as familiar household words. Rarely, if ever before, was it the good fortune of any ruler to be able to state so much truth, of such momentous import, in so few and fitting words. The inaugural is honest, simple, unaffected, truthful, patriotic, reverent, great. ... It will stand forever as an announcement, grand in its simplicity, and unflexible in its resolve, of the faith of the American people in the stability of their free government and the justice and invincibility of their cause. It will make thousands say, who have not hitherto said, 'God bless Abraham Lincoln.'"

On March 18, *Harper's Weekly* offered the following evaluation of Lincoln's speech: "The inaugural address of the President is characteristically simple and solemn. He neither speculates, or prophesies, nor sentimentalizes. Four years have revealed to every mind the ghastly truth that the Government of the United States is struggling in a death- grapple with slavery; and as a new epoch of the Government opens in civil war, its Chief Magistrate states the vital point of the contest, and invokes God's blessing upon the effort of the country to finish its work in triumph. With a certain grand and quaint vigor, unprecedented in modern politics, the President says: 'Fondly do we hope, fervently do we pray, that this mighty scourge of war may soon pass away.

Yet, if God wills that it continue until all the wealth piled by the bondman's two hundred and fifty years of unrequited toil shall be sunk, and until every drop of blood drawn with the lash shall be paid with another drawn with the sword, as was said three thousand years ago, so, still it must be said: 'The judgments of the Lord are true and righteous altogether.' We are especially glad that the inaugural does not, as the New York Tribune wishes it did, 'appeal to the rebels for a cessation of hostilities as pleadingly as its prototype (the first inaugural) urged forbearance from beginning them.' Such a tone would have been neither politic nor humane. When the President speaks of 'the progress of our arms upon which all else chiefly depends,' every man is reminded of the peace-history of the last year, and of the terms which have been constantly repeated, and which are perfectly well known to the rebels and to the world. Those terms are unconditional submission to the laws of the United States. We are equally glad that the President indulges in no observations upon Mexico, England, France, and things in general. He was taking the oath to continue the work in which his conduct has so satisfied the country that he is continued in his office by general assent. With a fine sense of propriety he says, in the gravest and most impressive way, that he accepts the trust and prays for strength to do his duty. And all true American hearts say, Amen!"

On the other hand, the *New York World* was not so kind: "It is with a blush of shame and wounded pride, as American citizens, that we lay before our readers to day the inaugural addresses of President Lincoln and Vice President Johnson. But we cannot hide the dishonor done to the country we love by withholding these documents from publication. They therefore must go forth to the country, such as they are. 'The pity of it, the pity of it,' that thus a divided, suffering nation should neither be sustained in this crisis of its agony by words of wisdom nor cheered by words of hope, but mocked at…by a…parody of 'John Brown's Hymn' from the lips of its chosen Chief Magistrate.'"

The *Chicago Times* was also not terribly impressed: "We did not conceive it possible that even Mr. Lincoln could produce a paper so slip shod, so loose-jointed, so puerile, not alone in literary construction, but in its ideas, its sentiments, its grasp. He has outdone himself. He has literally come out of the little end of his own horn. By the side of it, mediocrity is superb."

The *Brooklyn Daily Eagle* had a similar take: "Mr. Lincoln ... on an occasion when his utterances are eagerly looked for by millions of men, has nothing better to give us than a dissertation on the Providence of God, so crude and irreverent that it would be discreditable to a dull boy attached to an unpretentious orphan school."

Weeks after the inauguration, papers across the Atlantic would also weigh in. On March 25, the *London Spectator* remarked approvingly, "We can detect no longer the rude and illiterate mold of a village lawyer's thought, but find it replaced by a grasp of principle, a dignity of manner, and a solemnity of purpose, which would have been unworthy neither of Hampden nor of Cromwell, while his gentleness and generosity of feeling toward his foes are almost greater than we should expect from either of them. It seems to us...by far the noblest which any American President has yet uttered to an American Congress."

There were a number of photographs taken of Lincoln while he was making his speech, as well as drawings. On April 8, *The Illustrated London News* reported, "Our first Engraving shows the scene in front of the Capitol, on Saturday, March 4 - the reading of the President's address to the people assembled in the open street beneath the portico of that stately palace of the Federal Legislature. Mr. Lincoln himself will be at once distinguished. He is standing with a paper in his hand behind the small table on which a glass of water is placed; and the two gentlemen seated in front, a little to the left hand of the view are the ex Vice-President, Mr. Hamlin; and the new Vice-President, Mr. Andrew Johnson.... The reading of the address did not occupy ten minutes. It was received with loud acclamations; a salute of 100 guns was then fired, and President Lincoln entering his carriage, went home to his official residence, called the White House..."

There were tens of thousands of people in attendance on that day in March, and they also had a number of different opinions about the speech. Among those in the audience were a large number of soldiers who have received brief breaks in their fighting to attend the inaugural festivities. One of these men, General Isaac Sherwood, recalled, "I worked my way up through the crowd until I got within ten feet of Mr. Lincoln. He stood on a little platform, with a small table near him and on that a glass of water. He had a white pocket-handkerchief around his neck. I can see him now as I saw him then — a tall spare man, with deep lines of care furrowing his cheeks, a sad face, a strong face, the face of a man of many sorrows. I can hear him now as I heard him then, voice his last official utterance to the people of the United States: 'Fondly do we hope, fervently do we pray, that this mighty scourge of war may speedily pass away. With malice toward none, with charity for all, with firmness in the right as God gives us to see the right, let us strive to finish the work we are in, to bind up the nation's wounds, to care for him who shall have borne the battle, and for his widow and his orphan.' The mighty scourge of that war did speedily pass away. ... We were all tired of the war and that was the gladdest day that army ever saw. It was the proudest day any army had ever seen. We had fought the good fight, we had kept the faith and we knew that we would soon be in our homes again."

Another member of the audience, Edward Godkin, wrote about Lincoln's speech a few days later: "The President has been inaugurated, and has delivered what is, I suppose, the shortest "inaugural address" on record, probably for the best of all reasons — that he had very little to say. He has no new policy to trace out, nothing to explain that has not been already explained half-a-dozen times. In fact his real inaugural address was his last message to Congress, which was written immediately after his election, and was virtually his response to the country. What he said last Saturday was little more than a formal acknowledgment of the honor which has just been conferred on him, and though formal was hearty, but what is perhaps better still, and certainly rarer, it was in excellent taste. His English is about as good as Lord Malmesbury's, but he hardly ever says a feeble thing, and except when he undertakes to discuss questions of political economy, which are far out of his depth, he is invariably shrewd, if not wise. There is nothing in his state papers, admirable as they have been in many respects, so creditable, however, both to his head and heart, as the entire absence of all violence, either of language or opinion. I believe he has never once been betrayed into those paltry outbursts of passion and spite by which nearly everything that his Confederate rival says or writes is disfigured. Lincoln never attempts invective, and, although there is probably no living man who has been the object of more blackguard abuse, it has never, so far as I know, elicited from him a single expression of impatience or resentment."

A few days after the Inauguration, Lincoln wrote to newspaperman Thurlow Reed: "Everyone likes a compliment. Thank you for yours on my little notification speech, and on the recent Inaugural Address. I expect the latter to wear as well as — perhaps better than — anything I have produced; but I believe it is not immediately popular. Men are not flattered by being shown that there has been a difference of purpose between the Almighty and them. To deny it, however, in this case, is to deny that there is a God governing the world. It is a truth which I thought needed to be told; and as whatever of humiliation there is in it, falls most directly on myself, I thought others might afford for me to tell it."

In the end, there was perhaps no person in the audience that day to whom Lincoln's words meant more than they did to Frederick Douglass. He later wrote of his experience that evening at the Inaugural Ball: "Recognizing me, even before I reached him, he exclaimed, so that all around could hear him, 'Here comes my friend Douglass.' Taking me by the hand, he said, 'I am glad to see you. I saw you in the crowd today, listening to my inaugural address; how did you like it?' I said, 'Mr. Lincoln, I must not detain you with my poor opinion, when there are thousands waiting to shake hands with you.' 'No, no,' he said, 'you must stop a little, Douglass; there is no man in the country whose opinion I value more than yours. I want to know what you think of it?' I replied, 'Mr. Lincoln, that was a sacred effort.' 'I am glad you liked it!' he said; and I passed on, feeling that any man, however distinguished, might well regard himself honored by such expressions, from such a man."

Chapter 7: To Enter a New Era

"Lincoln began his final exhortation by asking all of America to enter a new era, armed not with enmity but with forgiveness. These words immediately became the most memorable expressions of the Second Inaugural. Quickly, in the short weeks left before his assassination, 'With malice toward none; with charity for all' became the watchwords written in newspapers, inscribed on badges. And after his assassination, they came to represent Lincoln's legacy to the nation. They would become some of our sacred words. Other words of his, from the Gettysburg Address—' of the people, by the people, for the people'— endure because they forever define America. 1 'With malice toward none; with charity for all' defined Lincoln's vision for a post–Civil War America. As Lincoln began this final paragraph, he had been speaking for barely five minutes. … Lincoln must have trusted that by now he had forged a bond with his audience. Well aware of their feelings of both hope and despair, he was about to ask his listeners for acts of incredible compassion. He would summon them to overcome the barrier of race and the boundary of sectionalism and come together again in reconciliation." - Ronald White

Lincoln in March 1865

One of the most important questions to answer about any speech is whether it accomplished what it set out to do. In that sense, Lincoln never got a chance to determine whether his second inaugural address hit its mark. As Garry Wills noted:

> "The end of the war was in sight — Lee would surrender at Appomattox a mere five weeks after the inauguration. But what would be done with that victory? Lincoln's appeal for latitude in the use of executive power, on the grounds that it was needed for waging the war, would lose all force when the guns fell silent. What new authority would he argue for to reach new goals? This was as thorny a situation, in its own way, as that which Lincoln had addressed in his lengthy First Inaugural. … If anything, the legal problems were even more complex in 1865. Would the Confederacy be a conquered nation? Or would it be a continuing part of America, in which some had committed crimes and others were innocent? How could the guilty be distinguished from the innocent, for assigning proper

punishments or rewards? On what timetable? Under whose supervision? Using what instruments of discipline or reform (trials, oaths of allegiance, perpetual disqualification for office)? And what of the former slaves? Were they to be allowed suffrage, indemnified for losses, given lands forfeited by the rebels, guaranteed work and workers' rights? The problems were endless, and the very norms for discussing them were still to be agreed on. Lincoln had his work cut out for him, and his audience could reasonably expect a serious engagement with matters that were haunting everyone on the eve of victory…

"The Second Inaugural was meant, with great daring, to spell out a principle of not acting on principle. In the nation's murky situation all principles — except this one of forgoing principle — were compromised. He was giving a basis for the pragmatic position he had taken in the Proclamation of Amnesty, which was deliberately shortsighted, looking only a step at a time down the long, hard road ahead. He defended that proclamation again in the last speech he gave, a month after the Second Inaugural. Speaking from a White House window to a crowd celebrating the war's end, he read carefully written words. 'I have been shown a letter on this subject [Reconstruction], supposed to be an able one, in which the writer expresses regret that my mind has not seemed to be definitely fixed on the question whether the seceded States, so called, are in the Union or out of it. It would perhaps, add astonishment to his regret, were he to learn that since I have found professed Union men endeavoring to make that question, I have purposely forborne any public expression upon it. As [it] appears to me that question has not been, nor yet is, a practically material one, and that any discussion of it, while it thus remains practically immaterial, could have no effect other than the mischievous one of dividing our friends. As yet, whatever it may hereafter become, that question is bad, as the basis for controversy, and good for nothing at all — a merely pernicious abstraction.'"

With the war nearing its conclusion, Lincoln faced the great question as to whether or not he really could implement his will with "malice toward none." When questioned about his plans for bringing the Southern states back into the Union, Lincoln told a crowd, "'I believe it is not only possible, but in fact, easier, to do this, without deciding, or even considering, whether these states have even been out of the Union, than with it. Finding themselves safely at home, it would be utterly immaterial whether they had ever been abroad. Let us all join in doing the acts necessary to restoring the proper practical relations between these States and the Union; and each forever after, innocently indulge his own opinion whether, in doing the acts, he brought the States from without, into the Union, or only gave them proper assistance, they never having been out of it.'"

Incredibly, the men who ensured Lincoln didn't have a chance to guide the country during

Reconstruction were at his inauguration. On April 24, 1865, in the wake of the president's assassination, New Hampshire politician Benjamin Brown French wrote to his son about a chilling incident. "I have little doubt that the intention was to assassinate the President on the 4th of March, & circumstances have been brought to my mind which almost convince me that, without knowing what I was doing, I was somewhat instrumental in preventing it. As the procession was passing through the Rotunda toward the Eastern portico, a man jumped from the crowd into it behind the President. I saw him, & told Westfall, one of my Policemen, to order him out. He took him by the arm & stopped him, when he began to wrangle & show fight. I went up to him face to face, & told him he must go back. He said he had a right there, & looked very fierce & angry that we would not let him go on, & asserted his right so strenuously, that I thought he was a new member of the House whom I did not know & I said to Westfall "let him go." While we were thus engaged endeavoring to get this person back in the crowd, the president passed on, & I presume had reached the stand before we left the man. Neither of us thought any more of the matter until since the assassination, when a gentleman told Westfall that Booth was in the crowd that day, & broke into the line & he saw a police man hold of him keeping him back. W. then came to me and asked me if I remembered the circumstance. I told him I did, & should know the man again were I to see him. A day or two afterward he brought me a photograph of Booth, and I recognized it at once as the face of the man with whom we had the trouble. He gave me such a fiendish stare as I was pushing him back, that I took particular notice of him & fixed his face in my mind, and I think I cannot be mistaken. My theory is that he meant to rush up behind the President & assassinate him, & in the confusion escape into the crowd again & get away. But, by stopping him as we did, the President got out of his reach. All this is mere surmise, but the man was in earnest, & had some errand, or he would not have so energetically sought to go forward…"

John Wilkes Booth is visible in the most famous picture of Lincoln's inauguration.

French was incorrect in his assessment of Booth's plans, but Booth and a number of other future conspirators were there that day. Today, Booth's assassination of Lincoln is often the only part of the plot that Americans remember, but as recently as November 1864, Booth's plan did not involve murder. When Lincoln brought Grant east and put him in charge of all armies, Grant, Sherman (now in charge out west) and the administration changed their military policies to one that resembled total warfare. The North's great advantages in manpower and resources would now be more heavily relied upon to defeat the South. One of the most important changes was that the Union stopped exchanging prisoners of war, a move clearly designed to ensure that the Confederacy would be harder pressed to fill its armies. Originally, Lincoln had opposed such exchanges, believing that giving wartime rights to the Confederacy implicitly acknowledged their independence, but they had been generally welcomed by both sides from almost the beginning of the war. Captives were exchanged and traded throughout the conflict's first few years. Exchanges were often not equal but were dependent on the rank of the soldiers being exchanged. For example, a captured general was exchanged for 46 privates. One major was worth eight privates, while a colonel was worth 15. The varying ranks of the soldiers, with privates at the bottom and generals at the top, allowed for different proportions of exchanges.

Ending the exchange eventually led to atrocities at prison camps like Andersonville and Camp Douglas in Illinois, but it had the desired effect of starving the South of able soldiers. Booth was particularly outraged by this, which many on both sides considered barbaric and contrary to the rules of warfare. In fact, generals on both sides still continued the exchange without informing their superiors.

It was this termination of prisoner exchanges that served as the motive for Booth's original plan. The North might not be willing to exchange soldiers, but Booth was sure they'd exchange for the President. Thus, Booth began gathering conspirators for a plot to kidnap President Lincoln and use him as a negotiating token to get back Confederate troops. Booth figured the President would be worth a great number of soldiers, which would give the rebels a potentially huge and much needed influx of men. A month before Lincoln's reelection in 1864, Booth took a trip to Montreal, which was a hotbed for Confederate espionage at the time, and he spent 10 days there. Historians are still unsure what exactly Booth did while he was there, but many have since speculated that he discussed kidnap plans with better connected members of the Confederate Secret Service and networks of spies.

In fact, kidnapping the president was still the plan when Lincoln's second inauguration took place on March 4, 1865. Despite his hatred of Lincoln, Booth attended the inauguration in Washington, and along with a crowd of over 50,000 spectators, Booth watched the president take the oath of office. The crowd also included several of his eventual co-conspirators: Samuel Arnold, George Atzerodt, David Herold, Michael O'Laughlen, Lewis Powell and John Surratt.

On March 15, the group met at Gautier's Restaurant at 252 Pennsylvania Avenue in Washington, just blocks from the White House. There, they discussed a plan to kidnap the President of the United States, send him to the Confederate capitol in Richmond, and hold him ransom until the Union released Confederate troops. Initially, the most realistic option for capturing the President would be to do so while he was in transit. This ensured that his security detail would be more limited than usual, and his travels were likely to be carried out in less densely populated places, ensuring minimal public awareness of the event. This would allow the group to scurry the President away to Richmond, where he could be held for ransom.

Two days later, on March 17, St. Patrick's Day, Booth learned that the President was going to head north to attend a play called *Still Waters Run Deep* at Campbell Military Hospital, located in the northern outskirts of Washington. Because Booth was a member of the nation's acting elite, he was privy to private information about public dignitaries, including the President, attending plays in the D.C. area, the very thing that made his plot possible the following month.

Booth informed his fellow conspirators, and they all agreed to go forward with the plan. Because the President's destination was known and his route could be reasonably assumed, the opportunity presented itself as the perfect one. The conspirators thus assembled along the President's route, hoping to intercept him along his way to the evening matinee. The sun was setting on Washington, providing cover to the conspirators in the darkened streets.

The conspirators were waiting for a man who would never show. To Booth's great dismay, the President had changed his mind and no longer planned to see *Still Waters Run Deep*. Instead, Lincoln attended a ceremony at National Hotel for the 140th Indiana Regiment, which was presenting its governor with a captured battle flag. Ironically, Booth was living at that very hotel at the time.

The Union capture of Richmond played a role in changing the plot from kidnap to murder. After all, Richmond had been the intended destination to bring Lincoln after the conspirators kidnapped him. Now, to Booth's horror, Lincoln was able to visit Richmond of his own accord. With the city under Union control, where could they bring the president?

Booth believed the war wasn't over, and to understand his rationale, it is important to remember that General Joseph E. Johnston, who Lee famously replaced at the head of the Army of Northern Virginia, still had a sizable army opposing General Sherman's army near the Carolinas. Although Appomattox is generally regarded as the end of the Civil War, there were still tens of thousands of Confederates in the field throughout April 1865, and Jefferson Davis himself was still holding out hope while fleeing from Richmond. Thus, Booth still intended to help the Confederacy somehow.

On April 11, Lincoln wrote, "And yet so great peculiarities pertain to each state; and such important and sudden changes occur in the same state; and, withal, so new and unprecedented is the whole case, that no exclusive, and inflexible plan can safely be prescribed as to details and collaterals. Such [an] exclusive, and inflexible plan, would surely become a new entanglement." That same day, Lincoln gave a speech at the White House in which he expressed his desire to give former slaves the right to vote, a policy that would come to fruition through the 13th, 14th, and 15th Amendments. Naturally, such a policy infuriated Southerners, and Booth was so enraged by the speech that he was later alleged to have claimed, "Now, by God, I'll put him through. That is the last speech he will ever give."

3 days later, Booth made good on that vow.

Bibliography

Angle, Paul McClelland; Earl Schenck Miers (1992). *The Living Lincoln: the Man, his Mind, his Times, and the War He Fought, Reconstructed from his Own Writings*. Barnes & Noble Publishing..

Basler, Roy P. et al., eds. (1953). *The Collected Works of Abraham Lincoln*. 9 vols. Rutgers University Press.

Fehrenbacher, Don E., ed. *Abraham Lincoln: Speeches and Writings 1859–1865* (Library of America, ed. 1989)

White, Ronald C., Jr. *The Eloquent President: A Portrait of Lincoln Through his Words*. New York: Random House, 2005.

Made in United States
North Haven, CT
12 September 2022

24003877R00072